From Power to Communion

FROM POWER TO COMMUNION:

*Toward a New Way of Being Church
Based on the Latin American Experience*

by
ROBERT S. PELTON, C.S.C.

with
Luis Calero, S.J.

Foreword by
The Most Reverend Ricardo Ramírez, C.S.B.

Afterword by
Paulo Evaristo Cardinal Arns

UNIVERSITY OF NOTRE DAME PRESS
Notre Dame and London

Copyright © 1994 by
University of Notre Dame Press
Notre Dame, Indiana 46556
All Rights Reserved

Manufactured in the United States of America

Library of Congress Cataloging-in-Publication Data

Pelton, Robert S., 1921–
    From power to communion : toward a new way of being
church based on the Latin American experience / Robert S.
Pelton.
        p.   cm.
    Includes bibliographical references and index.
    ISBN 0-268-00989-9 (alk. paper)
    1. Church.   2. Catholic Church—Latin America—
History—20th century.   3. Catholic Church—United
States—History—20th century.   4. United States—
Relations—Latin America.   5. Latin America—Relations—
United States.   6. Catholic church—Doctrines.   7. Pastoral
theology—Catholic Church.   I. Title.
BX1746.P385   1994
282'.7'09045—dc20   93-40435
                                                          CIP

∞ *The paper used in this publication meets the minimum requirements
of the American National Standard for Information Sciences—Permanence of Paper
for Printed Library Materials, ANSI Z39.48-1984.*

CONTENTS

Acknowledgments   ii

Foreword, by *the Most Reverend
Ricardo Ramírez, C.S.B.*   ix

Introduction   1

1. The Impact of the Latin American Experience
   on U.S. Religious   7

2. Strengthened Communion among
   Regional Churches   25

3. A Christian University at the Service of
   the Poor, by *Luis Calero, S.J.*   37

4. Small Christian Communities   63

5. Santo Domingo   79

Afterword, by *Paulo Evaristo
Cardinal Arns*   85

Index   93

ACKNOWLEDGMENTS

I am grateful to James R. Langford, director, University of Notre Dame Press; Jeannette Morgenroth, editor, University of Notre Dame Press; and Emmy Lou Papandria, for her years of service to the Church. I dedicate this book

To

Our Lady of Guadalupe,
Queen of the Americas

Father William F. Cunningham, C.S.C.,
who contributed strongly to inter-American relations
at the University of Notre Dame

Doctor Eleanor Taffae,
who taught me that there is power in communion

FOREWORD

The diocese to which I have been appointed as bishop encompasses an area of 47,000 square miles spreading across the border where the United States and Mexico come together, and where northern North America meets Latin America. "Border" translates in Spanish to *frontera*, which, for the ears of English speakers, immediately conveys the concept of "frontier." Frontiers in any part of the world are faraway places, far from the centers of official powers and official culture. Frontiers lie at the hinterlands of the mainstream. While rapid means of communication and travel have lessened the feeling of isolation in the frontier, geographical positioning still allows us to look at things somewhat differently. In our particular frontier we often look to the south of us, and this gives us a unique Latin American view of ourselves both as border people and as North Americans.

Latin America, and most frequently, Mexico, is very often in our daily thoughts, dreams, frustrations, and concerns. I lived, studied, and worked in Latin America for several years, and I have often felt that we in the northern part of our hemisphere simply do not give Latin America the attention it deserves. Nor do we fully appreciate the fact that a greater knowledge and appreciation of our neighbors to the south would be to our advantage as well as to theirs.

The five hundredth anniversary of the violent clash between Europe and the New World was remembered in
1992 and provoked healthy and much-needed research,
dialogue, and rereading of the relations between Europe
and North American on one side, and Latin America
on the other. Surely, more research and further debate
will continue in the coming years as we remember other
anniversaries. I foresee that there will be academic convo-
cations to commemorate and reassess the five hundredth
anniversaries of the arrival of the first groups of missioners, of Bartolomé de las Casas, of the first universities established in the New World, of the arrival and early work
in the Americas of religious orders such as the Dominicans,
Franciscans, and Augustinians.

But however deep our hope to explore and evaluate
history, we need also to give attention to present concerns.
One of them is that we might lose touch with our Latin
American neighbors as the Cold War ends and anticom-
munism becomes less of an excuse for North America to
be involved in Latin American affairs. Precisely because
communism no longer exerts the same threat as in the
past, we now have the opportunity to recognize Latin
America purely for its own merits, not for the threat that
the ideologies promoted there might be for us in the North.

Also, if democracy holds—and it is now more wide-
spread in Latin America than ever before—we might be
lulled into thinking that Latin America is now a set-
tled question. It is to be hoped that North America will
strengthen, not lessen, its interest in events to the South
as we in Canada and the United States seek new align-
ments and new issues that affect our hemispheric mutual
relations.

This book was written in order to keep the issues of
concern for both Latin and North America alive. It is
an attempt to help us in North America to learn from
the dramatic past few decades in Latin America. Among
the concerns that affect us mutually in the north and the

south, I would like to focus on the economy, the environment, drug traffic, the Latinization of North America, ecumenism, and the challenge of small Christian communities.

The Economy

Latin America captivated our attention during its great conflicts in the 1970s and 1980s. The years of the so-called national security policies, these decades were marked by violent revolutions, dictatorships, military oppression, the disappearance of thousands of people, and the dislocation of many others who had to leave their native lands as refugees. The 1980s are recognized as the "lost" decade where no economic growth occurred in Latin America and when there was constant pressure to pay foreign debts. Instead of moving forward economically, Latin America regressed to where it had been a few decades ago. Presently, it is still too early to say whether the North American Free Trade Agreement (NAFTA) will benefit ordinary people in both the northern and southern parts of our hemisphere.

For the ordinary people of Latin America, the foreign debt continues to be the source of their state of poverty. The people constantly ask themselves, "Who borrowed the money? For what was it spent?" and "How has it benefited our countries?" It is definitely time to renegotiate, reduce, and perhaps even eliminate some of the foreign debts that hurt our Latin American neighbors and, in the long run, hurt even ourselves in North America.

The Environment

The environment is a concern that all of us in the Americas share. The rainforests of Latin America are of crucial importance to the entire world, and we need to work together in order to preserve the precious and life-giving forested lands.

In November, 1991, the bishops of the United States issued a pastoral statement on the environment, *Renewing the Earth*.[1] In this statement we said that a moral challenge lies at the core of the environmental crisis. This challenge calls us to examine how we use and share the goods of the earth, what we pass on to future generations, and how we live in harmony with God's creation.

We, the peoples of the Americas, are witnesses to the environmental degradation that surrounds us: smog in our cities, chemicals in our water and food, eroded top soil, radioactive and toxic waste lacking adequate disposal sites, and threats to the health of industrial and farm workers. Poisoned water is an issue in both North and South America, and we all suffer as acid rain pours on all our countries. Greenhouse gases and chloroflourocarbons affect our entire earth and will continue to affect us for generations to come.

In our statement we call upon all people of good will to consider how to frame a common and workable environmental ethic. We are especially concerned about the poor and the powerless who most directly bear the burden of current environmental carelessness. "Nature will truly enjoy its second spring, only when humanity has compassion for its own weakest members." We need to understand that what happens in one part of our hemisphere will affect the rest, and for the sake of the survival of all of us in the Americas, the issue of the environment is a most compelling challenge.

Drug Trafficking

The demand and supply of drugs has to be another of those major concerns that we all share in the Americas. The people of Latin America who supply the addictions of the north continually remind us that they would neither produce nor sell harmful drugs if there were no demand.

Perhaps the root cause of addictions is related to our materialistic and consumer-minded society. People seem to be frustrated and unhappy with who they are and what they have. What consumerism tells them they are supposed to be, they are not. Neither do they have the things that are supposed to make them happy. If this is true, then the drug problem will not be resolved until we change our value system radically. And how this massive *metanoia* will happen is beyond me, but just because a problem is so immense does not mean that we do not do our best to analyze the root causes of this problem and develop strategies for how our moral educational processes can help us defeat the plague of drugs that affects so many of our people.

Latinization of North America

More a blessing than a concern is North America's gradual Latinization with the influx of more and more immigrants from the south. Both Canada and the United States appreciate immigration, and both our countries are proud that we are nations of immigrants and that it is immigrants who have lent their spirit of adventure, skills, enthusiasm, and ambition to contribute to the building of our countries. The Latinization of which I speak is no doubt happening more in the United States than in Canada, but the phenomenon is real. Already, Spanish is the second language of the United States. In California, for example, the minorities—and Hispanics comprise the largest of these—make up over 50 percent of the school population. In our own frontier region, our schools simply cannot keep up with the growing numbers of students coming from the south. Nonetheless, these new immigrants bring with them the values that we seem to be losing in the north. Family, faith, respect, a strong aesthetic appreciation, and a centuries' old continuity of culture—all

xiv   *Foreword*

of these things cannot but enhance the quality of North American civilization.

Efforts need to be made to create bridges of understanding and mutual appreciation between the Latinos of the North and those of the South. The Latin American heritage is such a rich one; it would be a cultural tragedy if those of us who belong to it were to lose touch with it. Likewise, Latin Americans need to recognize that their cultural brothers and sisters in the North have taken with them some of the best of Latin American traditions and values. We need to develop genuine pride towards one another.

Ecumenism

New ecumenical questions have arisen in Latin America. I often think that the effects of reformation are only now being felt in the Spanish-speaking world, as was bound to happen. Last year at an ecumenical gathering,[2] I pointed out that ecumenism for Hispanic Christians poses a formidable challenge. I have heard Latin American thinkers express a fear that Latin America may be heading toward the religious wars experienced in Europe during the sixteenth and seventeenth centuries. There have already been small skirmishes between Catholic and Protestant sectarian groups. In fact, strong animosities already exist between religious groups, and very little dialogue is occurring. At that ecumenical gathering, I suggested that a summit meeting of Hispanic Protestants and Catholics meet in order to begin some kind of dialogue, but since then I have discovered how delicate the relations are and that the summit meeting I suggested may take a good deal of time and effort. At this point, we do not have agreement even in terminology. For example, what for some groups is *evangelism,* for others is *proselytism.* For some freedom of religion means freedom to evangelize; for others, it means freedom from proselytism.

Small Christian Communities

In the past few decades the Christians of Latin America have contributed in a remarkable way to our understanding of Church. What is so striking is the interplay that has taken place between Latin American theologians and grassroots communities (*comunidades eclesiales de base,* CEBS, Christian base communities, or, more generally, small Christian communities). Latin American theology is generally a reflection on the real-life, often dramatic, experiences of the people in such a way that the Gospels take on a new and powerful dynamism. The Beatitudes, for example, come alive with an awesome vitality.

The bishops who attended the episcopal conferences at Medellín, Puebla, and Santo Domingo also have been thoroughly connected with the reality of the people of Latin America. They have struggled, sometimes agonized, in their yearning to respond prophetically to the voice of God in the poor and in victims of injustice.

The theologians of Latin America have powerfully and dramatically underscored that theology is a ministry and that the formulation of theology cannot be separated from the real faith and life struggles of people. The theologies of Latin America have legitimized the cry of the poor as a voice through which God speaks to all of us. In our day we have seen the dynamic power of God's word as it has come through the cry of the poor of those in Latin America who have been martyred for the sake of the kingdom of peace and justice (e.g., Archbishop Romero, the North American religious women, and the Jesuits of the Universidad Centroamericana). As Lutheran Bishop Medardo Gómez has said, "God through history has chosen to speak to the world through the suffering of peoples." Father Virgilio Elizondo says that the fullness of the paschal mystery is lived out in the crucified people of Latin America. The uniqueness of their witness is that in spite of their crucifixion they have not given in to cynicism or desperation, but have formulated a new existence based on authentic hope as inspired in the message of Jesus Christ.

The history of salvation teaches us that salvation often comes from totally unexpected sources. Out of today's people who suffer, salvation will come to the Americas. I am convinced that the contemporary western hemisphere will be saved by the spirituality of the martyrs of Latin America, by the indigenous peoples of our continents, and from those who in this century have suffered crucifixion. Those who have lived the cross will have the privilege to announce the resurrection. The poor of this hemisphere will provide us with a new and fresh understanding of the gospel and will spark life in the rest of us who all too often forget to feed the heart and soul.

This book is a welcome contribution to the growing literature that helps us in the mutual understanding between North and Latin America. But more than that, it helps us in our own understanding of ourselves as Christians in these uncertain and troubled days. I hope and pray that it will have the wide readership that it deserves.

MOST REVEREND RICARDO RAMÍREZ
Las Cruces, New Mexico
July 25, 1993, Feast of St. James the Apostle

Notes

1. *Renewing the Earth: An Invitation to Reflection and Action on Environment in Light of Catholic Social Teaching,* pastoral letter by the National Conference of Catholic Bishops, 14 November 1991 (Washington, D.C.: United States Catholic Conference, 1991).

2. "The Challenge of Ecumenism to Hispanic Christians," address by Bishop Ramírez, delivered at the NADEO luncheon in Denver, Colorado, 5 May 1992.

INTRODUCTION

The massive political and social upheavals of the recent past may well lead us to refocus our way of being Church. How we live, share, symbolize, embrace, and belong as Church may experience fundamental changes analogous to what we have witnessed in the former Soviet Union and in all of Eastern Europe. Dramatic ecclesial changes would similarly affect the whole world. A significant shift in ecclesiology is already under way in Latin America, and many changes in the Latin American Church may well signal new directions for the Church throughout the world. Particularly in the U.S., our way of being Church is taking many of the same paths as our brothers' and sisters' Church is Latin America. I think that our way of being Church will continue in the future to reflect and to be influenced by the Latin American experience.

An ecclesiology of communion has received since the Second Vatican Council an especially clear emphasis throughout the Church. The most recent official statement on it appears in a document of the Vatican Congregation for the Doctrine of the Faith, *Letter to the Bishops of the Catholic Church on Some Aspects of the Church Understood as Communion,* dated 15 June 1992. The Vatican statement on this ecclesiology pays attention to the interrelationship of Eucharist, community, and the role of bishops. Particular Churches are centered around the Eucharist and presided over by a bishop. The Eucharist is

1

the great sacrament of communion, and the papacy is the great symbol of unity.[1]

Since the Second Vatican Council communication has increased among regional Churches, even as they maintain their unity with the central Church. For example, Paulo Evaristo Cardinal Arns of Saõ Paulo, Brazil, states:

> The dynamism of participation and communion proposed by Puebla could be turned into a program not only for local Churches but also for a project of evangelization for the whole of the Third World, and for the relationship between this and the Churches of the First World. There is an increasing and widespread need for centers of participation and communion . . . in relations between the local Churches and their relationship to the unity of the universal Church.[2]

Such participation and communion take on particular significance in view of the fifth centenary of the Americas. In his "Five Hundred Years: A Faith Appraisal," Diego Irarrazaval says:

> Let us look toward the past, with a concern to strengthen the historical memory of peoples left in the lurch, but peoples resisting, and full of hope. Here are peoples who, apart from certain admirable exceptions, have been incorporated into modern nations and mestizo structures. Their current faith vision is not that of five hundred years ago. They believe in themselves (as before), but they also believe in striking alliances with other human beings. They have their religious characteristics, but they are also part of the Christian religion. They combine their own technology and wisdom with the techniques and knowledge of the hegemonic system.[3]

This type of inculturation implies a willingness to listen and learn as well as to contribute. Collaborative learning can be challenging both to regional Churches and to Rome. Such ecclesiology reflects the definite "growing pains" that are normal to any living growth process.

For example, as laypersons assume greater responsibilities, ordained ministers may feel threatened, and tensions can easily develop. While clearly respecting the role of ordained ministry, laypersons and clergy alike have a growing awareness of the importance of complementary ministries. In such circumstances, U.S. Catholics—lay and ordained—can make important contributions to the larger Church. In doing so, such Churches can move to a much stronger sense of interdependence, both among themselves and with other regional Churches.

Report 10 of the *Notre Dame Study of Catholic Parish Life* documents the high level of individualism of U.S. Catholics.[4] They reflect their own culture, particularly as described in Robert Bellah's *Habits of the Heart*. The same study points out that "core Catholics" (those with a basic commitment to the Catholic Church) are disposed to experience their Church in new and challenging ways. They are open to a new way of being Church, a Church that will celebrate and affirm the gifts of all.

This book reflects upon inter-American ecclesial interdependence and tries to discern what this implies for the future of the inter-American Churches. Along the way, I wish to point out the increased role of the laity. This role enables core Catholics to catch a few glimpses of the future.

Plan of the Book

We begin with the year 1961, when the Vatican requested U.S. religious communities to send 10 percent of their membership to Latin America during the decade of the 1960s.[5] Such candidates were to be chosen from "the best and most qualified vocations." The experience was to have a lasting influence upon the missioners and particularly upon those who returned to their own country as "reverse missioners." This proved to be an initial example of ecclesial interdependence.

Chapter 2, "Strengthened Communion among Regional Churches," describes the influence of the Medellín episcopal conference on the U.S. Church and in particular on the methodology employed at the 1976 U.S. Call to Action conference. The Puebla meeting of Latin American bishops in 1979 was also to influence U.S. observers in carrying out the mission of their own Church. During the 1980s this mission included a systematic reflection of the U.S. bishops on U.S. policy in Central America. This reflection eventually led to tensions between official U.S. Church leadership and the U.S. government. In turn, religious groups of various denominations began to establish links in a common cause of concern.

Next, a question is posed concerning the Catholic university of El Salvador: Can the University of Central America (UCA) serve as a model for Catholic universities in the U.S.? Can such a model of integrity—Christian, theological, and intellectual—be implemented in the United States? What can U.S. intellectuals learn from the martyrs of the UCA? What models for clergy-lay relationships are provided by the UCA experience?

These observations lead to an examination of the increasing role of the laity as exemplified in the small Christian communities. Richard Westley of Loyola University of Chicago predicts that in the future Church, "the parish will foster and facilitate the formation of many small intentional Christian communities, wherein people learn the skills of relating to their world in a liberating and unifying way."[6] In these communities the method of theological reflection has been strongly influenced by Latin American liberation thought.

The final chapter, "Santo Domingo," suggests new directions for the Church in the light of CELAM IV, the meeting of the Latin American bishops in the Dominican Republic in October 1992. Will inter-American pastoral contributions be strengthened? If they will be, how will this strengthening be manifested? What will be the kinds of relations between the Vatican and regional Churches of the Americas? How may we envisage the Church of the future?

Notes

1. *Origins*, 25 June 1992, vol. 22, no. 7, pp. 108–112.

2. *Tensions between the Churches of the First World and the Third World,* ed. V. Elizondo and N. Greinacher (New York: Seabury Press, 1981), p. 75.

3. This is part of a reflection presented to social communicators during their national meeting in Arequipa, Peru, 21 November 1989.

4. David C. Leege, "The Parish as Community," *Notre Dame Study of Catholic Parish Life*, report no. 10, March 1987.

5. See Gerald M. Costello, *Mission to Latin America: The Successes and Failures of a Twentieth Century Crusade* (Maryknoll, N.Y.: Orbis, 1979), pp. 47, 231.

6. Richard Westley, "In Defense of a Premonition," *Critic*, September 1991, p. 7.

1. THE IMPACT OF THE LATIN AMERICAN EXPERIENCE ON U.S. RELIGIOUS

On 17 August 1961, Monsignor Agostino Casaroli spoke in the name of the Pontifical Commission for Latin America at the Second Religious Congress of the United States, held at the University of Notre Dame. He appealed to U.S. religious superiors to send 10 percent of their membership to Latin America during the decade of the 1960s. He requested as candidates "the best and the most qualified vocations." This invitation, and the response to it, led to a radical change in the lives of many who became part of this experience. What follows are the stories of some of these persons.[1]

I selected at random eleven religious who responded to Monsignor Casaroli's invitation and asked them to share their recollections and insights about their experience. These women and men of varying ages and backgrounds served in different countries of Latin America. What they had had in common before they went to Latin America was their experience of the national Church in the United States.

Before the Second Vatican Council, the Roman Catholic Church throughout the world understood its role in a clearly institutional manner. In a special way, the Vatican and Monsignor Casaroli reflected the ecclesiology of that historical moment. The Church was seen as institution, with the key leadership emanating from the central authority of Rome. Casaroli enunciated a world vision of Church which was sensitive to the evident needs of the

Latin American Church. As in any human initiative, the
hand of God helped guide this development. Frequently,
this leads to surprises of the Spirit, as the lives of many
who responded to this call attest. The Church itself was
on the eve of a renewed—and biblical—way of looking
at itself as the people of God. This new understanding
of identity would challenge the entire Church, especially
those religious who left their homeland in the U.S. in order
to serve in a changing Church in another culture.

Many changes in the Latin American Church took place
during the short period from 1959 to 1969. These changes
affected religious communities at national and international levels. The dominant preconciliar model of religious
life was that of European communities. During the preconciliar period, structures of the religious life together
with the role of obedience received primary emphasis.
Stressing structure and obedience reinforced the vertical,
hierarchical style of authority. After Vatican II and before
the landmark Conference of religious leaders at Medellín
(1968), religious began to reach out in a more horizontal,
or collegial, manner of decision making. They gradually
became more aware of their lay sisters and brothers.

After the Medellín conference, religious of the continent began to respect much more the outward mission
of the Church. This led them to a deeper sensitivity to
the poverty that surrounded them. Communities began to
renew themselves, both in their lives and their missions,
with the result that they experienced the Church as the
people of God. This ecclesiological shift was to have a
dramatic impact on each of the persons I interviewed for
this chapter. By utilizing specific questions directed to the
respondents, we shall see how this ecclesiological change
reflected itself in their minds and hearts.

What Attracted You to Go to Latin America?

Seven of the men and women who went to Latin America soon after the Vatican's call went there precisely to

collaborate with the Church's desire to increase the presence of U.S. religious on that continent. There were specific variations to their response. Several of the religious had already taken an interest in Latin America, and one had had previous experience there. For most, however, Monsignor Casaroli's invitation itself created interest and sparked the desire to serve in this way.

As chair of the Department of Theology at Notre Dame, I heard in person and was moved by the address of Monsignor Casaroli. Before that, I had collaborated with John Considine, M.M., in promoting an interest in the Latin American Church by sponsoring a graduate course in the Department of Theology on inter-American relations.[2]

Margaret Houlihan, B.V.M., sharpened her initial interest in Latin America through a course taught by Luis Galvez at Notre Dame. Galvez and William Cunningham, C.S.C., helped her receive an OAS fellowship to Ecuador, where she spent many years in educational service.

Bishop Michael Pfeifer, O.M.I., had worked in Mexico earlier as a deacon. The 1961 call alerted him to the opportunity to return there as a missionary for sixteen years. During his years in Mexico, he was deeply moved by the spirit of community among the Latins, which has influenced his entire priestly life.

For Helen Battle, S.S.J., Sheila Salmon, H.M., Eileen McGovern, B.V.M., and Joseph Nangle, O.F.M., the 1961 invitation encouraged them and their communities to action, and they were among the first to respond to the call from the Vatican. Later, Judith Callahan, B.V.M., Theresa Gleason, B.V.M., Jo Ellen McCarthy, B.V.M., and Anne Hoban (formerly of Maryknoll) went to Latin America.

How Did Your Ideas of Church Change?

The common thread that runs through all responses is that emphasis on the Church as an institution changed to understanding the Church as the people of God. This implied a movement away from a top–down approach to discernment through a more communitarian reflection This shift took place through the lived experience of being Church with a focus upon community. Michael Pfeifer sensed this especially in family relationships. Anne Hoban grew in this awareness as she worked with small Christian communities in Chile. Eileen McGovern's emphasis on the sociological dimensions of community development influenced the shift in her own ecclesiology as she went back to Latin America to continue teaching. She and others were integrating their lived experience with a changing vision of Church. This process would lead them to a new way of understanding themselves and their Church.

As these religious were living a new way of being Church they were also influenced by official statements of the Latin American Confederation of Religious (CLAR):

> The Church as sacrament, so central in the texts of the Second Vatican Council, in which there is pointed out that the principal mission of the Church is not that of power and earthly greatness, but to be a sign of the community of persons between themselves and God. It is to be an instrument of peace, solidarity, and universal reconciliation. (CLAR 28)

———

> In this moment of our history many times our lives will be interlinked with a real solidarity with the poor and alienated of our continent. As we do this we are experiencing a process of conversion which draws us to enter into the poor's manner of thinking and feeling through living with them, and in participating in their struggle for justice with an evangelical spirit. (CLAR 14)

Such official statements would gradually influence the choice of ministries of the U.S. missioners, and, over time and with lived experience, their attitudes and approaches to their work in the Church changed significantly.

What Was Your Ministry?

Presently the Church pays close attention to inculturation, the process by which the Church becomes integrated in a local culture while retaining its own identity and bonds with other local Churches and the Church of Rome. It was not always so. It is significant that eight of the eleven respondents gave at least part of their time to formal teaching soon after their arrival in Latin America. Having taught in the United States, they assumed that they could make their best contribution in the classroom. These persons entered into educational ministries with generosity—but also with the assumption that they could easily move into a new culture. Were a similar situation to develop now, we would surely insist on a much stronger cultural and theological orientation for such missioners than we did then. In spite of their very clear good will, their lack of inculturation and their focus on the formal education of others implied that U.S. ministerial and educational approaches could be transplanted easily into Latin American soil.

Of those whose ministry was primarily or exclusively in the field of education, Margaret Houlihan became, soon after her arrival, the assistant director for the language institute at the Catholic university in Quito. Michael Pfeifer combined parish work with functioning as the director of a school and as a religious superior. Eileen McGovern taught at two universities, the Xaveriana in Bogota, Colombia, and later at the Catholic university in Salta, Argentina. Sheila Salmon taught nursing at the University of Chile and was on the staff in a residence for university women. For the greater part of my time in Chile, I was episcopal vicar for religious institutes in the archdiocese of Santiago, Chile; I also participated in a path-breaking diocesan synod in 1967–1968 and taught part-time at St. George's College and the Catholic university. Helen Battle combined her teaching in a high school and a normal school with pastoral education for lay catechists. Theresa Gleason in her teaching consistently showed a preferential option for the poor. Judith Callahan also combined work in several ministries, serving as a codirector in a vocational program for youth and teaching English, music, and art.

Only three of the missioners were active in noneducational ministries alone. Jo Ellen McCarthy did pastoral work in a housing project in Leon, Nicaragua. Even at that time she proved to be a valuable "bridge" through regular dialogues with religious from other Latin American countries, and she hosted visiting delegations to Nicaragua in its postrevolutionary moment. Anne Hoban worked directly with the Christian communities in Temuco, Chile, and ministered to youth groups in her parish. Joseph Nangle did pastoral work with indigenous persons in Bolivia; later he was founding pastor of a parish in Lima, Peru, where he endeavored to raise the consciousness of the affluent.

Each person contributed to the Latin American Church in a time of great change. However, even more importantly, all were left with a special imprint of that Church and returned to the United States to make genuine contributions to the Church here. Two significant influences from Latin America which can assist the Church here are the quest for community[3] and the preferential option for the poor. In addition, within the present Church in the United States are various cultural influences call for differing pastoral approaches.

What Did You Contribute?

The respondents were modest in terms of their perceived contributions while serving in Latin America. Even in this spirit, their sharing was quite revealing. For instance, Joseph Nangle spoke of his early efforts to communicate the meaning of liberation theology to the well-to-do of Lima. In his endeavor to introduce the affluent to these ideas, he showed Peruvian pastoral leaders that U.S. religious could act upon these insights. Helen Battle assisted people to become active agents in their own lives as she provided them with a new sense of God and the Church. Judith Callahan and Theresa Gleason encouraged youth, and particularly the poor, to continue their education. Both Michael Pfeifer and Anne Hoban tried to communicate in a new way God's love toward those whom they served. Eileen McGovern and Jo Ellen McCarthy encouraged a deeper social consciousness and in doing so presented another image of U.S. citizens. Sheila Salmon, Margaret Houlihan, and I assumed a learning stance in a different culture as we shared our professional expertise. In what these persons learned in Latin America, however, the most striking developments took place. All of us missioners received more than we gave. We were preparing ourselves—often without being conscious of it—to carry on a "reverse mission" to the sending Church. We have become missionaries to the Church in the U.S.

What Did You Receive?

Certain official statements of the Latin American Confederation of Religious (CLAR) provide an excellent background for what the respondents expressed as the benefits that they received during their years in Latin America. For instance, the document entitled *Religious Life in Latin America after Medellín* states that one example of spiritual growth is the acceptance and recognition of appropriate human friendships:

> In an institutional manner of understanding Church it is quite understandable for one to seek support and strength through a more direct dependence upon God. By contrast, the Church seen as the "people of God" leads us to recognize

the God-given gifts in each of us, and consequently to grow
in greater support one for another. (CLAR 28, p. 56)

This latter perception, based on seeing the Church as
the people of God, became the missioners' outlook, and
as it grew they developed bonds of friendship and interdependence. In the area of human affective growth, Michael
Pfeifer said that the Latin Americans "taught" him "the
real way to love and respect people." I agree; I became
aware of the importance of integrating in mature ways
the emotional and spiritual aspects of my life.

As the missioners deepened friendships—especially with
their Latin American sisters and brothers—they became
aware of the deep injustices that the Latins suffered. With
this growing consciousness, the missioners began to
sharpen the prophetic dimension of their religious calling. More and more often in the post-Medellín period,
they felt compelled to denounce such injustices, which
led to difficulties both within and outside the Church. A
CLAR statement expressed this reality: "This exercise of
prophecy does not only create tensions within the Church
and religious communities, but it also leads to persecutions
within society. This is the price that all prophets pay, and
that they will continue to pay" (CLAR 28, p. 59).

All of this would lead to a more explicit social and
political commitment of the religious, which in turn would
prompt a judgment of structures.

> The prophets knew how to judge civil and religious struc-
> tures confronting them with the revelation of God. . . . This
> prophetic role in relation to civil structures leads to a social
> and political commitment of religious. (CLAR 30, p. 47, *The
> New Spirituality of the Religious Life in Latin America*)

The religious also began to focus more clearly on their
role in a local or diocesan Church. As early as the arch-
diocesan synod of Santiago, Chile, in 1967, the missioners
appreciated better their need to address the pastoral priorities of their local and regional Church. This resulted

in many of them assuming apostolates that more directly concerned the poor. They were beginning to understand the meaning of an option for the poor.[4]

Thus, for example, Joseph Nangle and Eileen McGovern began a life-long commitment to the poor. For Helen Battle, this commitment led to a deeper political awareness and also (like Sheila Salmon and Theresa Gleason) eventually resulted in their questioning U.S. policies in Latin America. Their concern for the poor would eventually lead many former U.S. missioners in Latin America to painful disagreements with the policies of their own government. They would begin to experience some of the blessings of persecution even within their own country. And they are not alone; their prophetic commitment is shared by a variety of religious-based organizations that continue to exert influence upon inter-American relations (see the appendixes at the end of this chapter).

How Does the Latin American Experience Influence Your Life Now?

Eight of the eleven respondents report having developed a much stronger sense of social justice, and that this continues to influence them today. Such awareness includes participation in Amnesty International, legislative networks, and the sanctuary movement. They have not only become conscious of the role of the United States in inter-American relations but are also more sensitive to injustices within the United States. For a number of the missioners, their life-styles have become simpler due to the Latin American experience. Their awareness of Church continues to be flexible and broad. By leaving their own culture, immersing themselves in another culture, and then returning home, they now see things through a different perspective. In a number of ways they have become liaisons between the North American and Latin American cultures.

Are You a Bridge for Those Who Have Not Had a Latin American Experience?

Probably the best way to demonstrate that all of the respondents are in fact bridges between North and Latin America is to refer to their present activities and how some of these relate to Latin America:

Helen Battle, S.S.J. President of the Sisters of St. Joseph of Nazareth, Michigan. She is supportive of the sanctuary movement and various Central American advocacy groups.

Judith Callahan, B.V.M. Hispanic Ministry, diocese of Joliet.

Theresa Gleason, B.V.M. Counselor for Hispanic farmworkers in the United States.

Margaret Houlihan, B.V.M. For thirteen years the director of the Spanish language program for the archdiocese of Chicago. She now is a retired volunteer.

Anne Hoban. Works for the U.S. Census Bureau. She is actively involved in Amnesty International, and collaborates with the legislative action network of the Washington archdiocese.

Jo Ellen McCarthy, B.V.M. Coordinator for programs preparing persons for cross-cultural work.

Eileen McGovern, B.V.M. Psychiatric social worker. She meets personally with members of Congress to influence their decisions concerning Latin America.

Joseph Nangle, O.F.M. Formerly justice and peace director, Conference of Major Superiors of Men, U.S.A. He now works with Sojourners.

Robert Pelton, C.S.C. Director (emeritus) of the Institute for Pastoral and Social Ministry at the University of Notre Dame. I now direct the Kellogg Institute's Latin American/North American Church Concerns (LANACC).

Bishop Michael Pfeifer, O.M.I. The local ordinary of San Angelo, Texas. He works regularly with Hispanics.

Sheila Salmon, H.M. Program coordinator, Cross-Cultural
   Training Services.

Such ministries help these women and men to remain conscious of other cultures. At the same time it is important
for them to receive personal as well as ministerial support
in their efforts to deepen a new way of understanding and
living Church.

How Do You Receive Support for
Your Present Vision of Church?

Many respondents are supported in their present vision
of Church by like-minded persons who have experienced
a similar type of long-term immersion in another culture.
Anne Hoban, while no longer a Maryknoller, renews her
ecclesial outlook through regular contacts with present
and past members of Maryknoll. Others (Helen Battle,
Margaret Houlihan, and Judith Callahan) keep their mode
of understanding and living Church fresh through study
and by reading contemporary literature about Third World
issues. A number have entered into active membership in
advocacy groups such as Amnesty International, legislative
networks, the Coalition for Central America, etc. Others
deepen their sense of identity with the people of God
through their own present ministries: Jo Ellen McCarthy
serves as the coordinator for programs preparing persons
for cross-cultural work at Maryknoll, and Joseph Nangle
participates in the Sojourners' community. The women
have become more conscious of the pressing issues of
women, and they often seek out special support because
of this. Joseph Nangle has gone through a long process
of finding sympathetic listeners and support, to the point
where he is now sought out as a resource person on key
ecclesial issues of the Third World. I keep my vision alive
through both research and periodic trips to Latin America. None of our paths is easy because one can become

"sedated" by U.S. culture and forget one of the most significant experiences of one's earlier life.

How Do You Foresee the Church Thirty Years from Now?

A theme throughout the responses is that the Church, in God's providence and by force of circumstances, will be much more communitarian. Small Christian communities will be the moving force of the future Church. This will lead to greater egalitarianism—a clearer recognition of the gifts of all the baptized. In the U.S. Church, the Hispanic presence will be most significant. The ordained clergy—of different sorts—will express a bond between the hierarchy and grassroots.

None of this will be achieved easily. Some—particularly women—are frustrated with the present Church. For example, Anne Hoban predicts that "repression of women in the Church will deepen. So many of us have had positive experiences in business and government, where our only limits are those that are self-imposed." The sense of being devalued that lies behind the prediction of deepening repression deserves attention and appropriate responses.

Joseph Nangle, an experienced and wise missioner, makes an important observation for all to take seriously as we move into the future:

> If Catholics can somehow put up with the Institution, while seeking to change it, we shall have a Church which combines a wonderful grassroots in union with official leadership. Then the work of the Spirit will be respected at all levels of Church life.
>
> If we reject the institution and place ourselves outside of it—an understandable temptation—I am afraid that chaos will result. We who lived the Medellín moment in the Latin American Church can testify to the value of the institutional Church without denying her sins.

These eleven missioners, and the thousands who had similar experiences in Latin America, will be key persons in promoting the vision of a renewed Church that, I hope, will be a more purified and mature sign of God's presence on earth. Latin America certainly has returned the favor!

Questions for Reflection

1. Have religious in the U.S. begun to respect the outward mission of the Church more than they did twenty years ago? In what ways?

2. Have you known men or women religious who have returned from a missionary experience in Latin America and become missionaries to the U.S. Church? What do you see as evidence of this?

3. Joseph Nangle sees the Church at a fork in the road. Which road will U.S. religious take: Change the institution? Reject the institution? Give reasons for your answer.

Appendix 1:
The Washington Office on
Latin America (WOLA)

This summary of the activities of the Washington Office on Latin America (WOLA) is based upon a manuscript prepared by Virginia M. Bouvier: "The Washington Office on Latin America: Charting a New Path in U.S.–Latin American Relations." The complete essay is available from Latin American–North American Church Concerns (LANACC), 216 Hesburgh Center, Kellogg Institute, University of Notre Dame, Notre Dame, IN 46556.

The seeds for the Washington Office on Latin America (WOLA) were planted in the early 1970s when William Wipfler, then the head of the Latin American division of the National Council of Churches, and Thomas Quigley, of the United States Catholic

Conference's Latin American office, began to receive from the churches in Brazil wholesale reports of torture. These reports led to the establishment of a coalition of religious and civic groups, organized in 1974 to promote reasonable U.S. policies toward Latin America and to foster human rights, democracy, and social justice.

WOLA's birth was directly precipitated by military coups in 1973 in the two Latin American nations which had boasted the strongest traditions of democratic rule and popular participation—Chile and Uruguay. WOLA was an organization with a populist edge. Its founders believed that ordinary citizens had the right and the obligation to participate in the formulation of foreign policy decisions. The decision of the churches to fund WOLA marked a shift from prophesy to action. Initial funding came from the Protestant churches, and Catholic organizations added funds soon afterwards.

In the mid–1970s Joseph Eldridge, a Methodist pastor who had been serving as a U.S. missionary in Chile, became WOLA's second director, succeeding Diane La Voy, who had served for a short time. As the organization developed, it began to give attention to Panama and Central America. Soon, Panama, El Salvador, and Nicaragua were on WOLA's agenda. In 1978, Sister Jo Marie Griesgraber, C.P.P.S., became WOLA's first deputy director. She was instrumental in expanding WOLA's contacts with U.S. religious communities, particularly the Catholics.

WOLA went on to organize and assist numerous delegations to Latin America. Its actions related to the larger context of the political, social, and human rights conditions within which the electoral processes occur. The issue of police training illustrates WOLA's evolution as an institution. WOLA was able to work closely with individuals in Congress and in the press in order to influence appropriate legislation concerning police training and regularly kept its religious constituency informed of developments on Capitol Hill. By the 1990s, the 1974 prohibition against the U.S. training of police forces had been waived in favor of antinarcotics and antiterrorist police activities. Through its publications and work in grassroots coalition building, WOLA now hopes to galvanize the sort of church concern around U.S. drug policies that coalesced to oppose Reagan's Central American policy.

In the 1980s and 1990s there have emerged a plethora of ecumenical advocacy groups such as Witness for Peace, Network, the Religious Task Force on Central America, and the Center for Concern. Civic organizations such as Amnesty International, Americas Watch, and the Overseas Development Council have burgeoned.

WOLA has taken a leadership role in fostering the growth and development of a human rights community in Washington, and its strategies have looked increasingly toward greater collaboration with its Latin American counterparts. It has demonstrated considerable flexibility in shifting resources and priorities to accommodate the changing needs of human rights advocacy over time. As a case study, WOLA demonstrates how U.S. churches and individuals can give their southern neighbors more control over their own lives by providing greater opportunities for Latin Americans to engage in U.S. policy debates affecting their countries.

Appendix 2:
Religious-Based Grassroots Organizations

This is a summary of a fuller presentation of the subject by Edward Brett: "Religious-based Grassroots Organizations Working to Change U.S. Policy in Central America." A more complete version will appear in the November–December 1994 issue of *The International Papers,* available from LANACC, 216 Hesburgh Center, Kellogg Institute, University of Notre Dame, Notre Dame, IN 46556.

By the 1980s large numbers of U.S. Catholics and Protestants began to focus intently on Central America. The assassination of Archbishop Oscar Romero and the brutal rape and murder of four U.S churchwomen in El Salvador in 1980 were the catalysts that convinced thousands that violence was a daily occurrence in Central America and that U.S. aid played a part in its perpetuation. Over the next decade many people from a variety of religious denominations joined organizations dedicated to working for justice in Central America. For example there were the Witness for Peace, the Quixote Center, the Religious

Task Force on Central America, the Pledge of Resistance, Clergy and Laity Concerned, Share, the sanctuary movement, and Pastors for Peace. Other multi-issue social justice organizations, such as Pax Christi, Network, the Unitarian Universalist Service Committee, the American Friends Service Committee, and the Mennonite Central Committee, intensified their focus on Latin America. The Fellowship of Reconciliation and Bread for the World began to devote more time and energy to Central American concerns.

In the mid-1980s the Central America Working Group was created to coordinate legislative efforts in Washington, D.C. The Working Group also serves as a clearing house, disseminating the latest legislative news to grassroots groups throughout the country, thereby preparing them for local action. The crucial nature of the work is perhaps best illustrated, however, by its successful lobbying efforts in support of the Dodd-Leahy Amendment, which called for a 50 percent reduction in military aid to El Salvador. As Network lobbyist Richelle Friedman states: "The coordinating efforts of the Working Group are key to any success we have had on the Hill." Indeed, the observation of James McGovern, legislative aid to Representative Joseph Moakley of Massachusetts, bears this out. "The Church people who lobby Congress on Central America are much better organized today. They have become much more sophisticated in the methods they use to get their message across."

These religious groups have had both successes and failures. They played an important role in the U.S. government's decision in December 1990 to stop deporting undocumented Salvadoran and Guatemalan refugees. Likewise, they definitely helped to convince Congress to withhold 50 percent of the 1991 military aid for El Salvador. This was a major factor in pressuring the Salvadoran government to agree to the United Nations-mediated Peace Accords. Indeed, Robert White, the former U.S. ambassador to El Salvador, said that he believed that the work of religious groups, more than any other factor, kept the U.S. from invading Nicaragua in the 1980s. Most importantly, these groups have tried to walk with and learn from those who suffer in Central America. They have been transformed by them and, in turn, they are transforming many in their own churches and denominations.

Notes

1. Even though this chapter deals only with U.S. members of religious orders who went to Latin America, there also were many diocesan priests who served there. Some did this individually, representing their own dioceses; a number became associate priests with Maryknoll; others became members of an association of diocesan priests who serve in Latin America; The Society of St. James the Apostle. This society was founded by Richard J. Cardinal Cushing and it has had representatives not only from U.S. dioceses but also from other countries. It has had three hundred priest members. Cf. Gerald M. Costello's *Mission to Latin America* (Maryknoll, N.Y.: Orbis, 1979) for further details about U.S. contributions.

2. Father Considine later became the first director of the Latin America Bureau of the U.S. bishops, and also was a key person in the early development of inter-American Church relations. He was the person who suggested to the Vatican the 10 percent quota of U.S. religious in Latin America during the sixties. He continued as the director of the Latin America Bureau until 1968. See Costello, *Mission to Latin America,* pp. 47 and 231.

3. The *Notre Dame Study of Catholic Parish Life* (particularly report 10) shows how committed U.S. Catholics are seeking a deeper experience of community in their own parishes.

4. Pastoral synod, archdiocese of Santiago, Chile, *¿Que dices de ti misma?* (September 1967).

Suggested Reading

CLAR (Latin American Confederation of Religious). *Hacia una vida religiosa Latinoamericana.* Bogota, Colombia: Apartado Aereo 90710, 1987.

Cussianovich, Alejandro. *Religious Life and the Poor: Liberation Theology Perspectives.* Trans. John Drury. Ann Arbor, Mich.: Books on Demand UMI, [n.d.].

Fiand, Barbara. *Where Two or Three Are Gathered.* New York: Crossroad, 1992.

Leddy, Mary Jo. *Reweaving Religious Life.* Mystic, Conn.: 23rd Publications, 1990.

Schneider, Sandra M. *Beyond Patching.* New York: Paulist
    Press, 1991.
Wittberg, Patricia, S.C. *Creating a Future for Religious Life—A
    Sociological Perspective.* New York: Paulist Press, 1991.

2. STRENGTHENED COMMUNION AMONG REGIONAL CHURCHES

Vatican II and Latin America

No area of the world took the Second Vatican Council more seriously than did Latin America. The title chosen for the conference of Latin American bishops at Medellín, Colombia, in 1968 suggests this: "The Church in the Present-day Transformation of Latin America in the Light of the Council."

During the Second Vatican Council, dialogue began among inter-American Church leaders. This was best exemplified in the Catholic Conference of Inter-American Cooperation (CICOP). The organization was established in 1963 and existed until 1973 in order "to stimulate better understanding and friendship among Latin American and North American Christians." The objective of the annual conference was "that people would know and work toward effective inter-American action" concerning religious and socioeconomic themes. It made an important contribution to a better understanding among Christians of the Americas. After ten years, CICOP's activity was taken over by the regular meetings of the committee of inter-American bishops.[1]

By the mid-1970s communications between the official pastoral leaders of the Church in the United States and in Latin America were becoming more and more frequent

and increasingly focused on the area of social justice.
When the United States prepared for its bicentennial cel-
ebration in 1976, the president of the Catholic bishops,
Archbishop John Krol, designated the theme "Liberty and
Justice for All."[2] The staff of the United States Catholic
Conference (USCC) then assembled a distinguished committee of bishops, scholars, and other Church leaders to plan
a conference for the fall of 1976. As an example of inter-
American Church awareness, Father Bryan Hehir, then
director of the USCC Division of International Justice and
Peace, suggested in a memorandum that the 1976 conference take into consideration the 1968 Medellín Conference in which the role of the Church in society was
discerned.[3] The memorandum was sent to Bishop James
Rausch, the general secretary of the United States Catholic
Conference. The bicentennial discussion guide contained
several essays that were influenced by liberation theology.[4]

The 1976 Call to Action conference was to take a quite
different road, however. It did not become a Medellín-like
conference with emphasis upon the Church in contemporary society. Rather, eventually more attention was given
to internal Church issues. During 1975, teams of bishops
fanned out across the country for hearings in a process of
broad consultation similar to the methodology of the Latin
American Church. The conference was to become the first
national assembly of the American Catholic community
called by the bishops. The delegates were chosen primarily
by appointment of their local bishops. They were invited
to formulate concrete proposals for the Church, in view
of a subsequent five-year plan of action.

Criticism began to emerge as the process unfolded. One
complaint was that the procedures were being guided by
"romantic activists." This allegation was clearly rejected
by the nationally respected Monsignor George Higgins.[5]
Issues also surfaced that would result in later policy statements of the U.S. bishops, as, for example, the defense of

undocumented aliens from Latin America.[6] In a number of ways the Call to Action conference did not complete its original objectives. It took on a life of its own, while continuing to be influenced by Latin American Church developments.

An important example of the developments in Latin America that were closely followed by the Church in the U.S. and that influenced it took place in 1979 with the Puebla conference of Latin American bishops. This conference was an effort to critique the lived ecclesial experience during the eleven years after Medellín. What were the strengths and weaknesses of pastoral developments during this period?

Preparations for the Puebla conference were accompanied by concern lest the basic commitment of the Church to the poor of Latin America be reversed. There was also reason to believe that there were efforts to control the conference process and to reject liberation theology. In fact, Puebla did not reject the commitments of Medellín. Several themes of Medellín, such as the preferential option for the poor and the role of small Christian communities, were strengthened and achieved greater maturity. All in all, Puebla was a modest step forward.[7]

Archbishop John Quinn of San Francisco, president of the U.S. National Conference of Catholic Bishops, attended the Puebla conference. In reporting back to his U.S. colleagues, he suggested that the commitment of the Latin American bishops to a "preferential but not exclusive love for the poor" could serve as a model for the U.S. Church.[8] He also clearly encouraged more explicit participation in the public debate on U.S. policies in Latin America and the problems of undocumented aliens.[9]

Such support began to bear fruit in later policy positions of U.S. bishops. For example, Bishop Ricardo Ramírez said that he was "convinced that both the Medellín and Puebla conferences were a strong influence in our decisions to speak out on peace and economic justice issues."[10]

The U.S. bishops entered the Central American policy debate in a vigorous manner. They were aware that
the administration of President Reagan was encouraging regional military agreements and the staging of joint
war games involving U.S. and Honduran troops on the
Nicaraguan border. The bishops were becoming deeply
concerned with the potential for U.S. military intervention
in the region. Consequently, in congressional testimony
during the years 1980–1984, the bishops clearly supported
humanitarian aid to the region but opposed military aid
from any source.

In 1984 the tension increased between the U.S. government and the bishops. The administration called for a
fivefold increase in military aid over the next two years.
Bishop James Malone, then president of the USCC, pro-
tested in the "strongest terms" such an increase.[11] He
agreed that a precipitous cutback of U.S. military support
could result in chaotic bloodletting, but he still encouraged more forceful efforts on diplomatic and political
fronts. He was offended that the views of the U.S. and
Salvadoran bishops were "obviously not accepted" by the
Kissinger commission. These pastoral leaders identified the
core problem in El Salvador as "endemic social inequity
and brutal military oppression."

In 1985 the USCC testimony was directed explicitly
against aid to the Nicaraguan "Contras." There was also
growing criticism of the kinds of military equipment being
employed against civilian populations in El Salvador.

On 17 March 1986, Monsignor Daniel Hoye, general
secretary of the United States Catholic Conference, wrote
to the House of Representatives to oppose human rights
violations in Nicaragua, particularly those which restricted
the ministry of the Church. At this time he was also
supportive of the efforts of Archbishop Arturo Rivera y
Damas of San Salvador to reach a political solution of
the Salvadoran war and for his solidarity with arrested
persons representing humanitarian and Church groups.[12]

Later, on 22 December 1989, three Catholic leaders met with administration officials in the White House:[13] Archbishop Daniel Pilarczyk, president of the bishops' conference, and Cardinals Bernard Law and James Hickey. The administration representatives were White House Chief of Staff John Sununu and National Security Council Adviser Brent Scowcroft. The bishops urged efforts to bring about a cease fire and good faith negotiations to end the conflict in El Salvador. They were particularly concerned about the harassment of religious leaders in El Salvador and, above all, asked for an effective investigation concerning those responsible for the murder of six Jesuits and their coworkers at the University of Central America. This brutal deed was to serve as a linchpin in strengthening U.S. public opinion to resist a military solution to the Salvadoran war.[14]

Panama: An Example of Pastoral Leadership[15]

Very little media attention has been given to the internal Panamanian resistance of Roman Catholic leaders to the Noriega regime and how their opposition was morally supported by U.S. Catholic official leadership. Beginning in mid-1987 the Panamanian Episcopal Conference (CEP) sharpened and unified its pastoral vision of the whole problem. The CEP's statements of 17 June and 8 July 1987 formulated the guidelines for further declarations during three of the most challenging years in Panama's history. In these two statements the bishops spelled out their pastoral role in the midst of a political crisis and lamented the personal attacks by the media against some conference members. Soon, on 16 July, there followed a statement from the archdiocese of Panama criticizing the profanation of places of worship and the inhuman treatment of prisoners in the city jail. From this moment, the regime exerted more and more control and censure of the communication media every day. The Church's statements, read aloud at the Sunday masses, continued, however, to reach the people directly.

Then, on 3 August 1987, Archbishop Marcos McGrath, president of the country's bishops' conference, issued a public statement opposing the hostility being shown toward Jews in Panama. That same day the Panamanian Ecumenical Committee of Christian Churches pleaded for prayer and sacrifice in view of the increasing spiral of national violence. The tension grew when a handout was circulated from Noriega's political headquarters: "Wanted: Archbishop McGrath—Dead or Alive." This handout prompted two letters of support (4 and 15 September) for the archbishop from his priests. On 1 November the priests suggested that the Church offer to serve as a mediator in the national crisis.

On 26 February 1988, President Del Valle asked that General Noriega resign. Noriega refused and, in effect, deposed Del Valle. This action led to further efforts at reconciliation on the part of the bishops. On 29 March the bishops met with General Noriega, requested a clarification of the legitimacy of the executive authority, and asked that he step down. Their request was not acted upon. Then, the CEP proposed that Archbishop McGrath serve as peace mediator. On 6 April 1988, the Ecumenical Committee of Panama supported the proposal, and again the government had no response to the initiative. Instead, the authorities continued personal attacks against the archbishop and other Church leaders. On 2 May 1988 the CEP emphasized that the bishops spoke with one voice and that the Church would defer its offer of mediation for the time being because of the hostility of the government. In rapid succession there was concern expressed by the CEP to the government about the lack of freedom of some of the media of communication, the violation of the right to assemble, and the mishandling of civil and human rights.

On 5 April the CEP called for full and uninhibited participation in the coming national elections. The bishops approved a lay proposal for the careful monitoring of the national election, to be held Sunday, 7 May, as well as a first approximate tabulation based upon selected polling places throughout the country. On Monday, 8 May, the bishops announced the result of their sample tabulation: 72 percent for the opposition (Endara) ticket. Various international observers, including former-President Jimmy Carter, relied on this report in criticizing the procedures of the military government, which first attempted to alter the results and then declared the whole process void.

On 11 May, the CEP praised the exemplary conduct of the voters and strongly criticized the physical attacks on members of the opposition. On 9 May, Archbishop McGrath's house had been surrounded by troops, and some visitors to the house were assaulted and arrested. Most tragically, on election day in the town of Concepción, in the diocese of David, Father Nicholas Van Kleef, a Dutch Vincentian priest, while preparing to say mass for the people was fatally wounded by the Panamanian militia. The bishops from the entire country, as well as many priests and faithful, attended his funeral, despite military threats.

The Panamanian bishops as a team echoed an earlier statement of their martyred brother, Archbishop Romero: "To our brothers military, who have the strength of arms, we ask that you not use them against a defenseless people whose only arm is a strong will to live with dignity and in peace." The bishops' statement took on particular significance in view of the government's own nullification of the elections and the extraordinary tension which resulted. Once more, on 28 May 1989, Archbishop McGrath insisted that the Church wished only to facilitate national reconciliation: "Brothers and sisters: we are conscious also that we must be ministers of reconciliation; we will not cease to call and work for it."

Complementing these Panamanian efforts, on 8 June 1989 the Central American bishops issued a strong statement of support for their Panamanian brothers and sisters. They also urged the Organization of American States (OAS) to assume "a firm and decisive attitude in the case of Panama, insisting upon an end to the dictatorship there."

On 3 December 1989, the Panamanian bishops criticized a "double aggression," internal and external. The external was the enforced economic measures taken against Panama, principally by the United States, measures which were to stifle the Panamanian economy for years to come. The internal was the violence of imprisonments, the wounding and torture of citizens, and the lack of respect for human rights. The bishops expressed the deep disappointment of the Panamanian people in the totally ineffectual mediation attempted by the OAS.

The United States' invasion on 20 December created an entirely new situation. On 22 December the bishops published a note lamenting all that had provoked this severe blow to Panamanian identity and calling for a quiet return to legal, civil government in the whole country, with all necessary restitution.

On 26 December the CEP expressed its public support for the apostolic nuncio, Bishop José Laboa, who granted General Noriega asylum in the Vatican residence. They indicated that the granting of asylum brought to a conclusion the bloodshed there. Finally, they insisted that Noriega be turned over to justice while respecting his rights. Throughout the entire very difficult process the bishops of Panama remained faithful to their own mission. Their commitment was expressed well in the statement of the Rev. Edward Waldron (Episcopal pastor, Christ Church, Panama): "Of the four power sources in Panama—military, government, commercial sector, and Roman Catholic Church—the Church is the only fit arbiter of the nation's future. Indeed, it is the only power source showing genuine interest in the welfare of the people."

U.S. Episcopal Support for the Panamanian Church

U.S. Catholic bishops supported the actions of the Panamanian Episcopal Conference and of the nuncio, Archbishop Laboa, in granting refuge to General Noriega. Archbishop Daniel Pilarczyk, president of the National Conference of Catholic Bishops, stated: "I am convinced that the actions taken by the nuncio in Panama were intended to save lives and not to hinder the course of justice."[16] Archbishop Roger Mahony believed that attention should be shifted from General Noriega to the "broader questions regarding the future of the Panamanian people and their democracy and economy."[17]

Peace in El Salvador

On 16 January 1992, peace accords were officially signed in El Salvador. The cease-fire took effect on 1 February 1992. One important reason for this achievement was the constant effort of U.S. and Latin American Church leaders to seek together a peaceful solution to the bloody conflict. It is an excellent example of regional Church leaders listening and learning from each other. In this process there has been a strong emphasis upon human rights. The role of the Church in the peace process in El Salvador highlights the growth in communications among the pastoral leaders of the Americas that had become more frequent from the 1970s on, especially in the area of human rights.

Questions for Reflection

1. What effects have the conferences at Medellín and Puebla had on the thinking and actions of the bishops of the United States?

2. What evidence is there that suggests that the official thinking of the U.S. bishops leans toward "preferential but not exclusive option for the poor"?

3. Why has the U.S. government been slow to hear the bishops of Latin America?

4. In the near future will the dialogue between inter-American pastoral leaders extend into areas beyond human rights?

Notes

1. Ordinarily, the conference proceedings were published. For example, *Human Rights and the Liberation of Man in the Americas*, ed. Louis M. Colonnese, (Notre Dame, Ind.: University of Notre Dame Press, 1970); *Conscientization for Liberation*, ed. Louis M. Colonnese (Washington, D.C.: Division for Latin America, United States Catholic Conference, 1971); *Quo Vadis Latinoamerica . . . ?* P. Frederick McGuire, et al. (Washington, D.C.: Division for Latin America, Department of International Affairs, United States Catholic Conference, 1973, in Spanish). For background concerning CICOP and its transition into the bishops' meetings, see Thomas E. Quigley, "Age: 'Venerable'; Future: 'Uncertain,'" *Commonweal*, 2 March 1973, pp. 493–494. Quigley, who at the time of his essay was the director of the foreign visitors office at the National Catholic Welfare Conference (NCWC), also distributed privately a paper in March of 1973, "CICOP: After Ten Years," in which he encouraged a continuation of the meetings.

2. David O'Brien, *The Call to Action: A New Way of Doing the Work of the Church,* unpublished manuscript, Preface, p. 11.

3. Ibid., p. 72.

4. Ibid., p. 106.

5. Ibid., p. 127.

6. Ibid., pp. 16, 17.

7. Robert S. Pelton, C.S.C., "Puebla—A Modest Step Forward," the *Furrow,* June 1990 (see also a separate statement of the bishops, "A Message to the People of Latin America)."

8. *Origins*, 10 May 1979, vol. 8, no. 47, pp. 742–745.

9. Ibid.

10. Bishop Ricardo Ramírez, *Path from Puebla* (Washington, D.C.: United States Catholic Conference, 1989), p. 11. For a world Church impact of the Latin American Church, see *Born of the Poor*, ed. E. Cleary, O.P. (Notre Dame, Ind.: University of Notre Dame Press, 1990).

11. Statement issued on 8 Feb. 1984, by Bishop James Malone, then president of the USCC.

12. Statement published by the office of the general secretary.

13. *Origins*, 4 Jan. 1990, vol. 19, no. 31, pp. 502–504.

14. Arthur F. McGovern, S.J., "The Impact of Liberation Theology: A Personal Response," *International Papers in Pastoral Ministry*, April 1991, vol. 2, no. 2, p. 8: "Liberation Theology has been a primary, perhaps *the* primary, factor in awakening U.S. citizens to the grave problems confronting Latin America."

15. This summary of Panamanian Church developments is drawn from documents provided by the Panamanian chancery office on 3 Jan. 1990.

16. *Origins*, 11 Jan. 1990, vol. 19, no. 32, p. 519.

17. *Origins*, 18 Jan. 1990, vol. 19, no. 33, p. 538.

Suggested Reading

Boff, Leonardo. *Church, Charism, and Power: Liberation Theology and the Institutional Church*. New York: Crossroad, 1985.

Hastings, Adrian. *Modern Catholicism: Vatican II and After*. New York: Oxford University Press, 1991.

Legrand, Hervé, Julio Manzanares, and Antonio García y García, eds. *The Nature and Future of Episcopal Conferences*. Washington, D.C.: The Catholic University of America Press, 1988.

Reese, Thomas J., S.J., ed. *Episcopal Conferences: Historical, Canonical, and Theological Studies*. Washington, D.C.: Georgetown University Press, 1989.

Tillard, J. M. R. *Church of Churches: The Ecclesiology of Communion*. Collegeville, Minn.: Liturgical Press, 1992.

3. A CHRISTIAN UNIVERSITY
AT THE SERVICE OF THE POOR

Luis Calero, S.J.

The University of Central America

The 1976 bombing of the press at the University of Central America (Universidad Centroamericana, UCA) in El Salvador signaled the beginning of a violent turn of events by critics and opponents of the university. This criminal action, which badly damaged the building and equipment of the on-campus press, was followed by years of continuous attacks on school personnel and facilities. During the subsequent thirteen years the university suffered at least fifteen more bombings. Violence eventually escalated into the despicable massacre of six Jesuit priests, their housekeeper, and her daughter, on 16 November 1989. These actions were clearly intended to intimidate the school out of operation and to silence voices which kept speaking in defense of the country's poor majority. Such crimes, incomprehensible to us, accustomed as we are to the relative peacefulness of U.S. university campuses, reflected the outrage that this Catholic university evoked among some sectors of Salvadoran society.

Why had the UCA become so controversial? What could bring about such mindless actions against it? Some may claim that the university had become unwisely outspoken in a sensitive climate of great social and political volatility. Others may claim that El Salvador had become an endemically violent and repressive society with no tolerance for

the UCA's decidedly clear ideas on the need for change.
None of these explanations may sound satisfactory. They
need further elaboration. In this essay I would like to
provide insight into these questions by looking at the
genesis, growth, and outcome of El Salvador's history
of social inequity in light of the critical role that this
Jesuit-run university played in a society beset by moral
and political bankruptcy. My intention is to indicate the
appropriateness of the UCA's posture in defense of the poor
and to invite reflection on the challenge that other Christian universities may derive from this tragic and prophetic
experience.

First, I will provide some fundamental background of
the history of the country to help us understand the more
recent social crisis which led to the 1979–1991 civil war.
Second, I will discuss the impact that Vatican II and subsequent Latin American bishops' conferences had on the
Church, with special reference to El Salvador. Third, I will
explain the UCA's self-understanding as a Christian university and the nature of its insertion into what it called the
realidad nacional (the national social reality). And fourth,
I will offer some reflections on the applicability of the UCA
experience to other Christian universities, particularly in
the United States.

Economic and Social Background of the Crises

El Salvador was born out of a violent birth: an evolu-
tionary process of social and economic inequity. The origin of the civil war that raked the country during the last
decade, taking the lives of seventy-five thousand people,
goes back to the history of the accumulation of power and
wealth that began with the arrival of the Spanish in the
sixteenth century.

The European conquest led by conquistador Pedro de
Alvarado in 1524 radically altered the course of life for
native societies. The introduction of diseases to which

the natives had no immunity took a heavy human toll. El Salvador's estimated population of some five hundred thousand persons was reduced to 10 percent of its former size within a century, and half again after the Spanish invasion. The number of natives continued to decline during the greater part of Spain's three centuries of colonial rule.

With the native population significantly reduced and the social fabric of indigenous life debilitated, a relatively small number of Spanish settlers managed to overcome Indian resistance and to establish mechanisms of domination, particularly in regard to ownership and control of the land. In the beginning, Indian communal lands and the Spanish private hacienda coexisted side by side, with enough holdings for Europeans and their descendants and for the small number of Indians who had survived. Native labor was conscripted through the systems of *encomienda* and later *repartimiento* which placed allotments of natives at the disposal of the Spanish. The expansion, for export, in the cultivation of native cacao beans, balsam wood, and later añil (natural blue dye) created a new source of revenue for the European settlers. Cattle ranching emerged, particularly along the coast, in large landholdings where herds of cattle roamed freely, often intruding and destroying Indian crops. Tensions caused by Spanish appropriation of native land, the country's basic source of livelihood, exploded periodically into conflict that indicated the deep-seated dissatisfaction of growing numbers of people who had come to be dispossessed.

Thus the arrival of the Spanish in 1524 at Cuscatlán, part of what today is El Salvador, led to the disintegration of native life. Subsistence societies that had effectively managed the fragile tropical habitat on a sound social and environmental basis were incorporated into an economy of export which changed patterns of resource usage, production, consumption, and labor. This incorporation, although gradual, eventually destroyed the self-sufficient fabric of native life.

By the time El Salvador obtained its independence from Spain in 1820, and from Guatemala in 1832, the region was effectively controlled by a handful of families who managed the economic and political life of the country in very much a feudal manner. Labor was cheap and sufficient, land was controlled by a few, political power rested with the economic aristocracy, bringing wealth and political control under one and the same group.

The introduction of coffee during the mid-nineteenth century initiated a new chapter in the country that accentuated the already serious disparities between rich and poor. A coffee-based export economy allowed El Salvador to move from a marginal position internationally to one of greater economic articulation as Salvadoran beans gained acceptance abroad.

Coffee cultivation, however, was not possible everywhere in the country. It required the more temperate climate and richer volcanic soils of the central highlands which covered about one-third of the nation's territory. These fertile highlands, environmentally more apt for growing food crops such as maize and beans, had traditionally been the place of residence and work for the majority of El Salvador's population. As the coffee economy expanded, there was a pressing need to incorporate Indian and peasant communal lands (planted in subsistence crops) into the profitable business of coffee. Hacienda owners, entrepreneurs, and people with capital began to buy off this land or to expropriate it arbitrarily. Mechanisms for land expropriation varied a great deal. They included straight usurpation, economic and political pressures, and legislative action. The promulgation of the 1881 national law to abolish the system of communal landholdings was the last and major blow to traditional economies. The rise of a prosperous coffee industry which became central to El Salvador's national economy created a class of landless or impoverished peasants, some of whom became sharecroppers in coffee haciendas, some of whom were forced to move into the less fertile agricultural areas around the country.

By the turn of the twentieth century the picture of land ownership of this small nation had been so changed as to become unrecognizable. Campesinos and the few remaining Indian communities had been pressured out into marginal lands. Those who resisted were harshly punished. The landed oligarchy created strong security forces to protect their interests and to deal harshly with expressions of opposition, protest or revolt. This repressive machinery was financed largely by private coffee wealth. Clearly a system of private land ownership for export had replaced, at the expense of the poor, a system of communal land use for self-sufficiency.

The strong alliance between the oligarchy and the military became clear during an organized protest in 1932 when peasants from the coffee-producing states of Ahuachapán and Santa Ana in the north marched towards the capital city, demanding the return of their expropriated land. Fearful of a massive revolt, and before the masses reached San Salvador, the armed forces opened fire against the marchers, killing about thirty thousand men, women, and children in a senseless massacre that came to be known as La Matanza. The memory of this tragedy, brutal and aimed at the landless, has lived since in the consciousness of Salvadoreños. From the time of La Matanza any attempt to speak against the intolerable social conditions has been met with the brutality of torture, disappearance, and death.

The igniting of the civil war was the predictable outcome of internal political forces that could no longer be restrained and that were unleashed in the form of open conflict. Frustrated and unable to bring about substantial political reform in the country, the government's opposition formed a coalition of forces under the name FMLN (Farabundo Martí National Liberation Front) and took up arms to fight the entrenched oligarchy. The Salvadoran military, backed by U.S. weapons and advisers, responded in a butchery that massacred peasant villages where the FMLN was thought to operate or to enjoy the sympathies of local populations.

The United States, under the Reagan and Bush administrations, interpreted this conflict as a war between unreconcilable ideologies: totalitarian communism and free democracy. They refused to see the social and structural foundations of the problem. Approximately $6 billion were channeled by the Reagan and Bush administrations in the form of military and government aid, increasing the already intolerable level of human suffering.

The war caused pervasive destruction. Not only were tens of thousands killed and one-quarter of the population displaced by 1989, but the economy was shattered. The economic impact was especially great on the poor: real minimum wages in 1989 were 35.6 percent of their 1980 level. Not surprisingly, by September 1987, national opinion polls showed that an overwhelming 83.3 percent of the population supported an end to the war through a negotiated settlement. The economic and human costs had been too high. The lesson from the Central American war appears clear.

This conflict raises questions about the lack of foresight in U.S. perceptions regarding international affairs—and the causes for these misperceptions. By seeking the exclusion from political participation of broadly based movements on the left, the U.S. unleashed one of the most ferocious periods of repression in Latin America. It provided $1.2 million daily in military aid to the war against the FMLN. This assistance, which surpassed the entire country's earnings for coffee exports, did not prove capable of neutralizing or defeating the support for the rebel program. Instead, military aid fueled corruption as it supported a financially stable military class and failed to correct the army's brutality and constant violation of human rights. This war also demonstrates that support for multilateral negotiations can be more effective economically and less costly humanly than the unilateral use of force.

The Latin American Church after Vatican II

Much of the inspiration for recent changes in Latin American Catholicism stems from Vatican II and from the subsequent bishops' gatherings at Medellín, Colombia (1968), and Puebla, Mexico (1979). The council sought to address the Church's place and role in the modern world in the light of modern developments which, it was felt, needed to be attended to for an effective proclamation of the gospel. Traditional models of the Church as an unchanging and hierarchically ordered institution were challenged and replaced by a new self-understanding of the Church as the pilgrim people of God. The new model implied a changing and evolving community of Christians making their way through history, adapting to new circumstances and cultural change. The focus on change as central and desirable to the Church's self-understanding provided Christians with a new impulse to define themselves in accordance to the signs of the times and in relation to the social, political, and economic order of the latter part of the twentieth century. In Vatican II, the Church welcomed the need for change and the legitimacy of action and involvement as constitutive for Christian life.

The Medellín conference of Latin American bishops was convened for the purpose of understanding and implementing the spirit of Vatican II in Latin America, where the majority of the world's Christians live. The directives of the Council were read against the background of the region's drastic problems, particularly its overwhelming poverty and political repression.

Perhaps Medellín's most significant contribution was to characterize unjust social systems as structurally sinful and as reflective of institutionalized violence. Traditional

Christian notions of sin, which in the past had emphasized personal morality, were expanded to include entire social systems built on inequality. In sociological terms, Medellín treated poverty as structural in origin, not simply as the result of personal failure or human incompetence. This insight sharply reduced the value placed on traditional approaches to charity since it was clear that misery and injustice could not be eradicated by charity alone. The bishops at Medellín insisted that structures causing poverty had to change, and that this change required power and political action. The years that followed Medellín were marked by much debate and conflict as various sectors of the church increasingly became active in denouncing structures of sin and privilege that kept Latin America's majority poor.

When the Latin American bishops gathered again at Puebla, eleven years later, they set out to assess the experiences learned since Medellín and to plan the course of action for the future. Puebla dealt, among other things, with the rapidly expanding phenomenon of grassroots church organizations known as *comunidades eclesiales de base* (CEBs, small Christian communities). These small groups, which sought to read Scripture and reflect on its application, were the logical outcome of the Church's invitation that the laity play an active role in the transformation of unjust structures of society. In some places CEBs supplanted the more traditional expressions of folk religion, such as pilgrimages, processions, and local devotions. While CEBs received acceptance at Puebla, the bishops worried about having control over them so that their participation was in line with Church teachings.

Puebla is often identified with the phrase "preferential option for the poor." This phrase, first coined by Latin American liberation theologians, insisted that just as God had made a preferential option for the marginal in salvation history, so Christians were called to do the same today. The poor represented a special locus of God's love, a love which nevertheless was not exclusive of others.

Thus, in discovering and appropriating the experience of the poor, Christians were not only exposed to sociological data but confronted with the action of God in history.

Medellín and Puebla greatly raised expectations in the Latin American community as the Church appeared to be willing to let go of its former privileged status. In post-conquest Latin America the church had emerged as one of the strong powers that tailored social and political life, its influence extending quite beyond the realm of religion. For almost five hundred years, in some countries more than in others, the institutional Church had become closely aligned with government and ruling elites whom it regarded as defenders of Christian order and values. During this time the Church largely accepted the social order as a given, encouraging charity work as the way of responding to the needy but not questioning the root causes of oppression and poverty. It saw disparities but felt that they were unresolvable results of the natural evolution of society.

Vatican II led to a self-examination. The Church in Latin America questioned its traditional role in a society marked by offensive disparities. It raised questions regarding the roots of dehumanizing poverty and offered itself, with its moral and institutional weight, to join in the project of social and economic transformation. The bishops spoke about the structural causes of poverty, of "structural sin," and acknowledged that the very foundations of Latin American civilization rested on principles diametrically opposed to the gospel. In challenging the past, the institutional Church was not only recognizing its historical complicity with systems of oppression but also making itself available to the new task of building the kingdom of God upon justice.

The Church's new posture was received with surprise, enthusiasm, and skepticism. Skeptics were proved wrong. Christians, both Catholic and Protestant, moved along with commitment and relentless enthusiasm to bring the gospel into the public sphere and reshape society. In Chile, Christians participated actively in the presidential campaign that elected socialist President Salvador Allende (1970–1973), and they later tirelessly denounced the ruthlessness of General Augusto Pinochet, who ousted Allende in a coup d'etat that initiated a period of terror that included the torture, death, and disappearance of thousands. In Brazil, Christians, through the CEBs, created a new critical ferment of change that was instrumental in bringing an end to military rule and the beginnings of a fragile civilian democracy. In Nicaragua, Christians were vigorous participants in the Sandinista revolution which overthrew the long and hated Somoza dynasty, redistributed land, and began the reconstruction of a more egalitarian society. In El Salvador, Christians—as workers, teachers, peasants, and priests—challenged centuries of oppression and domination by a small landed elite and its military supporters. Skeptics had underestimated the inner strength and dynamism of Latin American Christians who under prophetic leadership had the power to move, not mountains, but structures in society.

In El Salvador, as in other Latin American nations, the directives of Medellín and Puebla gradually had an impact. Religious orders of men and women studied these directives in the light of their special charisms and planned strategies for change. Some groups abandoned the traditional schools where they had taught the children of the elite, others reshaped their institutions to respond to social needs, and many moved into the barrios to live among the poor. In 1975 the Jesuits held their thirty-second general congregation in Rome, a significant landmark in their history, and issued an unmistakable mandate for all Jesuit works: the service of faith and the promotion of justice. The inseparability of Christian faith and transformation of society had been made clear.

In 1977 Bishop Oscar Arnulfo Romero was appointed as archbishop of San Salvador, the capital city of a much troubled nation. Civil war formally broke out in 1979. Known for his moderate and conciliatory political views, he was expected to direct the Church cautiously through a difficult time without rocking the boat. A few months after the archbishop's appointment, Fr. Rutilio Grande, a Jesuit and close friend of Romero, was gunned down along with two coworkers of his rural parish as he drove down a country road. This was, biographers claim, the turning point for Romero. With the death of his friend and the growing suffering of his people, it became clear to him that the road ahead was that of unwavering defense of the poor. He understood that his friend had been murdered because he had spoken with the voice of thousands of Salvadoran peasants who clamored for justice. From that point on, Romero became a tireless and fearless defender of his flock, alienating many of the powerful. In his Sunday radio sermons, heard by friends and enemies alike, he analyzed the state of the country, denounced violations of human rights, and called all Christians to join in the common task of halting the killings and respecting human life. He himself was shot to death by a sniper while celebrating mass in a hospital chapel on 24 March 1980.

In Bishop Romero, the Church in El Salvador entered a new phase in its history as it made explicit the meaning of its preferential option for the poor. The man who had been appointed to guard safely a tradition of trust between church and state became the strongest critic of government and a tireless advocate for social change and for an end to privilege. His saintly presence and moral authority ignited the hearts of the poor, who claimed him as their own. The Jesuits at the UCA, more and more aware of the prophetic and critical role that the university was to play in this conflict, found inspiration in Romero as friend and shepherd. A sentiment of fraternal unity emerged that brought the university's support to the bishop and the bishop's unyielding commitment to the poor to the university.

The Distinctiveness of the UCA
as a Christian University

The UCA's beginnings are significant. Like Bishop Romero, who was changed by contact with the people, the UCA also underwent conversion. The UCA's early years were far from prophetic. The school was founded in 1965 at the request and with the support of members of the economic elite in order to protect Catholics from the evils of communism and secularism that were considered rampant at the country's national university, the only major university in the country at the time. The UCA's mission was to educate upper-class youths and to protect them from becoming radicalized in the highly political atmosphere at the national university. The school was entrusted to the Jesuits since they supposedly offered the desired qualities of intellectual rigor, academic discipline, and theological orthodoxy. Ironically, Colonel Rivera, the rather benevolent military dictator at that time, presided over the solemn opening of the university. The list of those who attended the inaugural ceremony reads like a social register of a high-society wedding in San Salvador.

In time, the UCA came to question and reject the mission of safe refuge under which it had been founded. Within a few years it chose the path of active participant in the events of the nation rather than of silent observer and loyal friend of the status quo. Because of its reinterpretation of its mission, it earned the dislike and even hatred of some of its former trustees and benefactors. For some, the university betrayed its original inspiration; for others, its new self-understanding signaled the inevitability of change and transformation that had to arrive sooner or later when the school opened its eyes to the social reality outside itself. Some insisted that the Jesuits had become Marxist revolutionaries while others praised them for joining the work of justice in the construction of the kingdom of God.

The role played by Christians in El Salvador and at the UCA during the last twenty-five years would appear unthinkable to anyone in the pre-Vatican II Church. It is the story of new awakenings out of uncritical dormancy and sinful complacency into the fertility of grassroots Christianity and, by default, into martyrdom. Sister Ita Ford, Bishop Oscar Romero, and Father Ignacio Ellacuría (to name three martyrs in this awakening) symbolize the transformation of a once-stagnant Latin American Christianity that evolved into a source of human liberation. The UCA was born in sin and was changed by a saving grace mediated by the poor.

The issue of the UCA's Christian distinctiveness raises two interrelated questions: one of identity and the other of applicability. In the first place, we want to know if the UCA offers a model of a university which is distinctively Christian, that is, an academic institution truly grounded in the values of the gospel. In the second instance, we want to find out the degree to which this model, if found worth imitating, is applicable to Christian universities elsewhere—particularly in the United States.

I believe that the UCA was successful in becoming a distinctly and authentically Christian university, not just a professional institution. As a university it made its goal the search for truth, but as a Christian university it derived this truth from the spirit of the gospel. How did it do this? Puebla, when speaking about the mission of Latin American Christians, emphasized the centrality of the preferential option for the poor. According to its teaching, the poor provide the lens through which reality is to be understood and faith is to be lived. What this means is not always clear. In the case of the UCA the experience of the poor provided the organizing principle that nourished and directed the life of the school. The experience of the poor, which is one of suffering, illuminated the path toward becoming a truly Christian university.

The UCA expressed this idea by stating that its mission was to study, understand, and transform the *realidad nacional*, the national social reality. This ontological data was nothing but the reality of poverty, oppression, and persecution under which the majority of Salvadorans lived. In other words, poverty and the poor constituted the *realidad nacional*. The UCA identified its mission by exploring avenues of knowing, interpreting, and changing the massive and pervasive experience of human suffering. It also used its social leverage to transform it. This approach placed the entire university at the service of the marginal, without abandoning the specific tasks of professional education which were proper to the university. Solidarity with the poor became the foundation on which the life of the university was based. The school, in its multiple activities, became a voice for those who had no voice.

Making a preferential option for the poor did not mean turning the university into a theological or pastoral center. In fact, the department of theology was and continues to be a rather small part of the school. During the time of the war the UCA continued normal academic operations preparing students in various fields and disciplines, but always trying to provide a comprehensive view of the structural sinfulness under which the nation lived. University members who were dissatisfied with this approach left the school altogether, others became so politically engaged that they had to go underground or were forced to leave the country for safety, and most continued to ponder where they belonged. But clearly the leaders of the UCA had made a preferential option for the poor by placing the university and its available resources (people, classes, publications, forums, library facilities, research centers) at the service of society's most pressing needs. Students were taught to understand that their Christian mission went beyond acquiring professional skills in their field, and that as Christians they were asked to join the struggle for human dignity. Some did. Others did not.

The UCA also understood that a Christian university's mission could not stop with the education of members of the university community, particularly students, but rather it was called to reach out into the larger arenas of the country and the world. This is, I think, the great genius of the UCA. In a society where the distortion of truth was commonplace, where people were arbitrarily accused and killed for "being communists," the UCA saw its mission as educating a broader public in the meaning of truth. It became a vehicle for providing the perspective of the poor to anyone in that wider audience who was willing to listen to another version of the story—different from what the Salvadoran government, the military, and the U.S. State Department had to say.

The UCA spread quite creatively its knowledge about the national reality to the entire country and to many corners of the world. Its press published hundreds of articles, journals, and books dealing with a broad range of subjects regarding national social conditions. Publications included commentaries on the New Testament, studies on refugees and the displaced of the war, denunciations of human rights atrocities. Many people throughout the country and abroad either read these writings or heard about their content, and in this way they became informed. The UCA also created a national debate forum known as *cátedra nacional*, possibly the only wartime platform where opposing views, in a highly polarized society, had an opportunity to be heard. Out of this came the growing realization that reason, not weapons, was the more intelligent way of dealing with a war that was bleeding the country to death.

The UCA was keenly aware not only of its Christian role but of its character as a university. It understood well that it was not a political party, a parish, or a human service agency. Universities are educational centers of research and learning. Consequently, the UCA, as a Christian university, addressed the plight of the poor in several ways that were fitting to its character as a university.

First, it established three competent research institutes and think tanks for the study of the *realidad nacional*. They were the Human Rights Institute (Idhuca), the Center for Documentation and Information (Cidai), and the Opinion Polling Institute (Iudop). These centers deliberately focused their work on issues directly related to national social life, providing a scientific perspective on structural issues. They dealt with questions of distribution of income, land reform, refugee problems, gross violations of human rights, etc. In so doing, the institutes provided the scientific backbone to help understand the root causes of the conflict and to propose viable solutions. Each institute published a journal in which their studies were made accessible to the public. The UCA, a relatively small school with limited resources, placed a great deal of emphasis on research and writing for the education of the national public.

Another dimension of the UCA's involvement as a university came through the leverage of its leaders. Through the mass media, Father Ellacuría in particular gained a high profile nationally, speaking on behalf of the poor, denouncing the intransigence of the military, calling for restraint, dialogue, and reform. Throughout the world his voice carried a message of truth accompanied by his critical insight and moral authority. Other leaders did the same, each in their own capacity, so that the struggle of El Salvador would become similarly well known. Last but not least the university's theological center (today known as Centro Monseñor Romero) trained seminarians, lay catechists, delegates of the word as leaders of a Church committed to the poor. These lay leaders became leaven in their own communities, and many were killed by right-wing death squads for their "subversive" work of preaching the gospel of justice. This was becoming "the hour of the laity."

The UCA's distinctiveness rested on its ability to bring together faith and reason, with assertiveness and without apologies, confident that one could nourish the other.

Faith demanded the recognition of God's action in the struggle of the simple. Reason provided scientific tools of analysis to understand this struggle and to present strategies for change. Father Ignacio Ellacuría put it well when he said:

> In the Christian university reason and faith merge, therefore, in confronting the reality of the poor. Reason must open its eyes to the fact of suffering. Faith, which sometimes is scandalous to those without it, sees in the weak of this world the triumph of God, for we see in the poor what salvation must mean and the conversion to which we are called. (Commencement address, Santa Clara University, 12 June 1982)

The study and teaching of truth came accompanied by the denunciation of falsehood. In the line of disclosing lies, the UCA played its most critical, difficult, and prophetic role—a role that caused agony, since people knew that denunciations were frequently followed by bomb attacks. The UCA raised the unwavering and eloquent voice of truth to denounce openly and squarely the perpetuation of an ethically unbalanced system based on lies. In a country where everyone feared for their lives, and where the slightest public criticism constituted a serious offense to warrant condemnation and bullets, the UCA spoke courageously about structurally based suffering. It believed that only truth and the destruction of falsehood could eventually restore life. This transparent commitment to the poor, and to those who joined their plight, caused periodic bombings and ultimately the killing of the university's leaders. Their massacre was abominable, but it was also the highest tribute to the people to whom they had devoted their lives.

In sum, the UCA placed itself at the service of the poor, not necessarily in the sense of bringing the poor into the classroom but rather in the sense of transforming the university into an institution which alerted and educated society about the unacceptable and intolerable human conditions which prevailed in the country. In the process of

making its university resources available for those strug-
gling for justice, it brought an innovative relation between
the academy and Christian faith.

Applicability of the UCA Model
to Other Christian Universities

The UCA unintentionally developed a model for being a
Christian university which is universal in scope. This of
course does not mean that its experience and way of pro-
ceeding can be literally reproduced or transplanted from
this war-torn society to any Christian university elsewhere
in the world. We must keep in mind that the UCA's response
was unique because the conditions to which it responded
were unique. The historical antecedents, conflict players,
and successive events in the drama before and during the
civil war belonged to El Salvador alone. There is, however,
a sense in which the experience out of which the UCA
emerged is universal. Dehumanizing poverty, oppression
and domination of certain groups, deprivation of basic
rights—these are all traits of contemporary culture that
are present in various degrees everywhere we turn. Thus,
the specific social reality of war in El Salvador was unique,
but the general social reality of poverty and oppression is
general in the world, affecting even societies with high
standards of living like the U.S.

Because of this commonality of social and economic
conditions, and because of the shared principles to which
Christian universities subscribe, we can think of the UCA
model as enlightening for the work of other academic
institutions. This is particularly the case for Christian,
and more precisely Catholic, universities in the United
States. We share a common tradition and purpose in the
larger life of the Church. The experience of the UCA invites
us to grow in our distinctively Christian roots which in
the contemporary context means making a deliberate and
preferential option for the poor. How do we do this? By

inserting the university into the national and global reality, and by directing our academic resources into changing structural injustice.

I assume that any university is planted in a society in crisis because we are a world in crisis. I also assume that the populations that are most critically affected by crisis are those that are economically poor. No Christian university today can claim to exist outside a historical context of dehumanizing social forces. The role of the UCA was contextualized by a society of profoundly uneven distribution of resources, domination of a powerful economic class supported by a corrupt military, and a resulting civil war that uncontrollably destroyed human life. We in the United States also exist in a society characterized by great gender, racial, and socioeconomic disparities. Moreover, we live in the one nation that remains today as world superpower and whose political behavior and decisions affect life-and-death issues all over the world. We also know some of the major problems: on our planet composed of over five billion people, one-fifth, including ourselves, lives in plenty, one-fifth lives in destitute poverty, and the remaining three-fifths are able to get by. We have pushed the earth's productive capabilities to their limits and, in this process, eliminated vital resources for the survival of our world. The gap between rich and poor nations has widened since the early 1980s, affecting most especially Africa and Latin America. Our own country contains only about 6 percent of the world's population but consumes close to 40 percent of the world's resources. The list goes on, and the picture of the future that emerges is indeed bleak.

What does this have to do with our reflections on the UCA? It means that we have to root our educational mission, as the UCA did, in the framework of needed structural changes and concerns. If the work of a Christian university is to be grounded in the gospel by making a preferential option for the poor, we need to turn our attention to impoverished groups and defenseless environments. If we define our mission as the study and teaching of truth, critically and intelligently, we need to find ways to have an impact on drug-infested neighborhoods and the destruction of tropical forests.

From the example of the UCA it should seem clear that assessing the results of Christian education by classroom teaching evaluations and the number of books and articles published, is simply not enough. Rather, academic effectiveness also has to be measured by the impact that the institution has on the national and global reality. A Christian university stands for academic excellence, but this excellence must address the structures of a world in crisis. We need to link the Christian academic endeavor to the transformation of society, otherwise we are just one more university in the pile. A good scholar not only publishes in recognized journals but directs his or her scholarly task into improving the quality of life.

Compared to universities of similar size in the United States, the UCA lacks the human and material resources considered indispensable for the efficient running of a school. Given budget constraints proper to a Third World country, it has few full-time faculty members, its libraries are insufficiently equipped, many of its laboratories are outdated. Only a fraction of the school's professors have a Ph.D. degree or its equivalent. Professional programs often lack technological tools or diversified instruction. Buildings could use some paint and repair. In some classes students may have to stand up during classroom lectures because there are not enough chairs. The UCA may look physically and academically modest to us, certainly understaffed and undersupplied. Yet one is struck by the impact that this unpretentious school has had on the recent life of the country, certainly disproportionate to its size and means. A school's social impact does not depend necessarily on the abundance, or even adequacy, of the goods it possesses but rather on its vision and commitment.

The UCA challenges the vision that places Christian universities on the same footing with the big research schools. Research institutions tend to be ethically and politically detached, interested in science for the sake of science, one or more steps removed from the structural reflections that lead to change. They inform the world but see themselves as indirect vehicles of transformation. To them the search for truth and justice is relegated to the realm of ethics and religion, and the denunciation of evil is handled by politicians and social activists. Falsehood is an area of quarrel for the courts, perhaps, but not of concern for institutions of higher learning.

In the U.S. tradition, universities are repositories of academic freedom, where a plurality of opinions may be reasonably expressed with respect and without fear of reprisal. The exchange and familiarity of contrasting ideas is seen at the heart of constructing a healthy academic life. It is relatively rare, however, to find an exchange of views that may lead to commitment and action, particularly in favor of society's underserved. Our academic life stops at the doorsteps of theorizing and speculating, right before we enter into the house of praxis. Catholic universities have, for example, found it difficult to come up with creative ways of teaching and implementing the U.S. bishops' concerns expressed in the pastoral letters on peace and on the economy. There seems to be a distance between Church hierarchy and Christian academia, even when we seem to find rare moments of theoretical agreement. At times it appears that we are more concerned with making the list of best college buys rather than offering a distinctively Christian education that challenges the system. The lesson from the UCA stresses that there is no opposition between being academically sound and prophetically alive—and that this combination holds the promise for the future of Christian university life.

First World universities may feel ill at ease with a school that espouses an unequivocal value system in defense of the poor and marginal and becomes an outspoken critic of structures of oppression. Academic civility in the western tradition establishes that we do not overstep boundaries that clearly delineate a distinction between reason and faith, knowledge and engagement. In this respect U.S. universities may look at the UCA with respect and admiration, praising the lives and work of individuals who have made a great and courageous contribution in the history of their country. By the same token they also feel that the character of U.S. academia is qualitatively different and that the UCA model, if acceptable for a society at war, is far from adequate for their own situation.

I am afraid that we have created a system of Christian universities that are run like conglomerate business corporations. To make them financially viable we have to make a profit and to train students for profit. The struggle for economic solvency overcomes our best intentions in being distinctively Christian, even if we want to be. If little is distinctive about the work and mission of Christian schools, if our task is focused on remaining competitive and training professionals adequately for a good slot in the job market, then we are defeating the purpose of bringing faith values to academia for the improvement of society. The task of training professionals can be done quite adequately and less expensively by larger, economically well-endowed, research institutions.

At Santa Clara University we have developed a way by which our own students get to know the reality of the wider community, particularly the underserved in the area. It is known as the Eastside Project—the name refers to East San Jose, a poor section of town where most of our students go to work. Through this program, students work in a placement or agency where they interact with a variety of different people, such as immigrants, senior citizens, hearing-impaired children, the homeless. The assignment given to students in these placements is an integral component of a curriculum course. Attending the placements is connected to experience in the classroom. For example, a cultural anthropology course may require that students interact with newly arrived immigrants in order to understand their experience of acculturation. Students in psychology may work with a group of hearing impaired children to study their process of learning. Thus, the placement is not a "service" task but rather an academic exercise which enables the students to enter, through the tools of a given discipline, into a world which otherwise may remain unknown to them. In this way they are confronted with the reality that lies beyond our peaceful campus and are challenged by it. This experience often marks the beginning of a student's life of concern and deeper commitment to changing structures.

Latin America Returns the Favor

Just as the UCA's press was repaired and stayed in business after the 1976 bombing, the UCA has survived the tragedy of the November 1989 massacre. Violence and insanity were crippled in the face of truth. The university managed to recover and grow from physical and moral destruction, like a plant that sprouts after a fire. Much of this repair work has been the result of the tremendous solidarity expressed by other academic institutions, governments, churches, and people of good will. Most importantly, the present-day strength of the UCA rests on the unbroken and resilient spirit of Salvadorans who continue to struggle for justice and peace.

Critical knowledge when applied to social systems is a dangerous tool. When knowing is directed towards exposing the inhumanity that strips rights and dignity away from people, it frequently arouses a desire to change and revolt. Education becomes an instrument that penetrates the roots of an unjust order, produces dissatisfaction, and demands reform. This may explain why some societies prefer not to educate their citizens or manage to downplay structural questions. Education empowers the poor to take charge of their lives and effect change. The UCA stands as an example of using knowledge for understanding the causes of poverty, for freeing people to become protagonists of their own lives, and for bringing to light mechanisms that keep individuals under domination. Raising structural questions about what keeps people subjugated proved to be dangerous. Knowledge directed towards the understanding of injustice caused panic among those who held the structures of power.

The genius of the UCA was to focus its educational endeavor on seeking truth and bringing together fertile minds, the gospel, and a close scrutiny of the concrete social reality. Through this formula it became possible to uncover the dishonesty of a system of privilege and to provide a voice to those enduring interminable hunger and unbearable abuse. In a world geography course that I teach at Santa Clara University, we discuss world hunger and poverty. I remind my students that thirty-five thousand persons die of hunger or hunger-related conditions every day, about six times the number of students we have in our school. Most of these deaths could be prevented if we appropriately handled social and environmental systems with knowledge, compassion, and justice. Some students are struck by these staggering figures and want to do something right away, while for others this is just one more statistic before their lunch break. Here is our challenge as a Christian university: to awaken understanding, to form consciences, to have an impact on *la realidad.*

Questions for Reflection

1. It is often stated that El Salvador's twelve years of civil war (1979–1991) were the inevitable consequence of centuries of social, political, and economic oppression. Do you agree with this statement? Explain your reasons.

2. The Latin American Church went through a substantial transformation after Vatican II. Outline the main conceptual changes introduced by the bishops' conferences in Medellín and Puebla. In your opinion, which of these changes led to the emergence of a "new Church" and the consolidation of a distinctly Christian university (UCA) in El Salvador?

3. Review the history of your personal formal university education and indicate if you find elements espoused by the UCA as part of your own process of learning. How would you alter your university education to make it have a greater impact on national and global reality?

4. In your view, what are the main obstacles preventing U.S. Christian universities (particularly Catholic) from becoming institutions at the service of the poor? What changes would you introduce?

5. Design a U.S. liberal arts undergraduate program in peace and justice studies that would integrate features of the preferential option for the poor in the curriculum. Be specific about the structure of the program, courses, requirements, topics of study, experiential learning, etc.

Note

Father Luis Calero, S.J., is Assistant Professor in the Department of Anthropology/Sociology at Santa Clara University, California. He is also a regular visiting professor at Universidad Centroamericana (UCA), El Salvador.

Suggested Reading

Brockman, James R. *The Word Remains: A Life of Oscar Romero.* Maryknoll, N.Y.: Orbis Books, 1989.
Browning, David. *El Salvador: Landscape and Society.* Oxford: Clarendon Press, 1971.

Edwards, Beatrice, and Gretta Tovar Siebentritt. *The Repopulation of Rural El Salvador*. Boulder, Colo.: Lynne Rienner Publishers, 1991.

Ellacuría, Ignacio. *Veinte años de historia de El Salvador (1969–1989)*. 3 vols. San Salvador: UCA Editores, 1991.

Ellacuría, Ignacio, and Jon Sobrino, eds. *Mysterium Liberationis: Conceptos fundamentales de la teología de liberación*. 2 vols. San Salvador: UCA Editores, 1991.

Gorostiago, Xabier. "New Times, New Role for Universities of the South." *Envio*, July 1993, vol. 12, no. 144. Managua, Nicaragua.

Hassett, John, and Hugh Lacy. *Towards a Society That Serves Its People: The Intellectual Contributions of El Salvador's Murdered Jesuits*. Washington, D.C.: Georgetown University Press, 1991.

Montgomery, Tommie Sue. *Revolution in El Salvador: Origins and Evolution*. Boulder, Colo.: Westview Press, 1982.

Sobrino, Jon. *Resurección de la verdadera iglesia*. San Salvadore: UCA Editores, 1989.

Sobrino, Jon, and Ignacio Ellacuría. *Companions of Jesus: The Jesuit Martyrs of El Salvador*. Maryknoll, N.Y.: Orbis Books, 1990.

White, Alastair. *El Salvador*. Westport, Conn.: Praeger, 1973.

Whitfield, Teresa. *Paying the Price: Ignacio Ellacuría and the Murdered Jesuits of El Salvador*. Philadelphia: Temple University Press, forthcoming.

4. SMALL CHRISTIAN COMMUNITIES

> In today's world there is a vocation to small Christian communities. The laity are the leaders in responding to this call.
> —*Bishop Christopher Mwoleka*
> *of Rulenge, Tanzania*

The Theological Roots for Small Christian Communities

Christian Duquoc finds in small Christian communities "the empirical form" of two fundamental principles of liberation theology: the prophetic role of the poor in proclaiming the shape of the future, and the identification of messianic hope with the cause of the poor."[1] Therefore the future rests not with those who "conquer" but with the oppressed who proclaim a new history without margins. Proponents of liberation theology believe that the future will be determined by the creation of a world without winners and losers.[2]

Liberation theologians eliminate neither Jewish messianic hope nor Christian hope founded on the Cross.[3] They find a continuing tension between these two poles. The basic communities seek ways to render this tension creative rather than destructive.

The Origins of Small Christian Communities

Much has been written about the origins of small Christian communities.[4] *Comunidades eclesiales de base* (Christian base communities, CEBs) began in Brazil (Barra do Pirai diocese) in 1956 as "Sunday services without priests." In 1963 they were initiated in Panama (San Miguelito parish in the archdiocese of Panama). They were perceived as a creative pastoral effort supported by the bishops but emerging from local grassroots laypersons. Many observers interpret the process of the communities' emerging as God's Spirit calling forth the many gifts of the people of God. Independently, three areas of the Catholic Church in the Third World—Latin America, Asia, and Africa—have experienced the strong growth of small Christian communities in recent times.

From Chicago to Panama

Father Leo Mahon of the archdiocese of Chicago did excellent work with Hispanics in Chicago. He served as the diocesan representative to Spanish-speaking Catholics. In 1962 Mahon and a team were sent to serve in the archdiocese of Panama.[5] Other diocesan priests became members of the St. James Society begun by Richard Cardinal Cushing of Boston. These volunteers were to serve in various dioceses of Latin America. The cardinal believed that this generosity would also bring blessings to the Church of the United States.

The Chicago team went to a barrio in Panama where the people lived in tar-paper shacks with no running water. The team had not brought a pastoral plan with them, but they were influenced by the community organizing methods of Saul Alinsky of Chicago. Mahon formed an organization called the Christian Men of San Miguelito, the special feature of which was a direct approach to Latin men, who usually regarded religion as only for women and children. Although these first efforts were not successful, it was from these failures that the team began to discover better approaches.

In a particular way they entered into dialogue with the men in a version of the Cursillo. From this group experience they gradually developed credit unions as a basic means for the self-help of the people. It took a long time for Church people to discover this new way of experiencing Church. This discovery occurred when small groups of laypersons began to commit themselves to faith building in communities. Three basic principles were emphasized: the need to form a living Christian community; an increased role of Scripture; and the centrality of the gift of prophecy. The people of San Miguelito experienced a fresh evangelization as they progressed in this new way of being Church.

Reverse Mission

In January 1971 Leo Mahon began to bring back to Chicago the fruits of his Panamanian experience, including the formation of small faith communities inspired by Scripture. Pastors in the area of Edgewater Beach and Rogers Park invited him to give a retreat. This was followed in subsequent years by other invitations, and in 1975 he decided that it was time for him to return permanently to Chicago.

Two laypersons, Richard Westley and Ethel Westley, were strongly influenced by Mahon and his new pastoral methodology. They guided a series of parish workshops on the formation of small groups, about which Richard Westley had preached and published for over twenty years. In his latest book he says:

> Our hope for the future of humankind and its habitat, the earth, lies not with the great and the famous, not with world leaders or international bodies, but with little people . . . who

cluster in small groups all over the world to unleash the power of love in their world.[6]

The Westleys were to contribute in a continuing way in sectors not economically deprived. Usually the persons in these sectors were white and of northern European descent. Small communities of middle-class people were developing. At the same time, there was a powerful movement coming from Latin America which was to influence strongly the growing Hispanic Church in the United States.

Evangelization of Hispanics in the U.S.

One example, among a great many, of evangelization projects among Hispanics in the U.S. was begun in September of 1973 in Coachella Valley, 110 miles east of Los Angeles and 125 miles northeast of San Diego. The project was started under the leadership of Father Joseph F. Pawlicki, C.S.C., of the Indiana province of the Priests of the Holy Cross, at the invitation of Bishop Leo Maher of the diocese of San Diego and with the approval of Father William M. Lewers, C.S.C. provincial. Bishop Maher desired in-depth missionary work to be carried out among the Hispanics of the Valley. Father Pawlicki had worked earlier as a missionary, both in Texas and then in Chile. An apostolic plan was developed that included direct evangelization and the formation of small Christian communities so that Hispanics would become missionaries to their own people.

Twenty years later, on Saturday, 18 September 1993, a fiesta was held—by one thousand persons belonging to sixty small Christian communities in the Valley Missionary Program at their headquarters, the Hispanic Cultural Center of Coachella. This project of evangelization has clearly been blessed by God and can serve as a model for other, similar efforts in the United States.[7]

The Hispanic Presence

In 1972 the First National *Encuentro* (encounter, meeting) of diocesan bishops and their delegates, took place in Washington, D.C. It was sponsored by the United States Catholic Conference (USCC) to begin to elaborate the content of a pastoral plan for Hispanics. This prepared the way for the second encuentro, held at Trinity College in Washington, D.C., from 18 to 21 August 1977, at which strong stands were taken to foster small Christian communities. A call went out to develop leaders for these communities, persons who would promote the growth of communities and thus revitalize the Christian lives of Hispanics.[8] On 12 December 1983, the National Conference of Catholic Bishops (NCCB) issued a pastoral letter, *The Hispanic Presence: Challenge and Commitment,* which shared the significance of Hispanics in the Church, called for a third encuentro to be convened, and pledged themselves to a national pastoral plan for Hispanic ministry.[9]

At the third encuentro, thousands of people involved in Hispanic pastoral concerns participated in a process of consultation and priority setting, which were the issues and content of the discussions that took place during the 15–18 August 1985 event and celebration. Once again participants committed themselves to the formation of small communities. They saw as more important than ever an ongoing theological and pastoral education for the formation of these communities.[10]

One of the responses to this need was the convocation of a national symposium on small communities sponsored by the NCCB/USCC Secretariat for Hispanic Affairs at the Center for Applied Research in the Apostolate (CARA) in Washington, D.C., 4–7 May 1989. The participants shared their American experience of small Christian communities and developed a historical context and constitutive

elements for small communities, to be published as guidelines by the U.S. Catholic Conference.

In the spring of 1994 the Bishops' Committee for Hispanic Affairs of the NCCB published a general guideline for
the American experience of small Christian communities
in the Hispanic community. The guidelines were accompanied by a bilingual video and study guide. This "how-to"
manual needs to be complemented by ongoing formation.

U.S. Small Christian Communities: Anglos/Hispanics

Gradually in the United States the growth of small
communities in the Church—both Hispanic and Anglo—
became perceptible. The communities began to "insti-
tutionalize" themselves in organizations to support and
complement each other. This was especially evident in a
National Consultation on Small Christian Communities,
which took place at the University of Notre Dame from
30 September to 3 October 1990.

The gathering was hosted by the Institute for Pastoral
and Social Ministry at the university in collaboration with
the North American Forum for Small Christian Communities, an organization of diocesan representatives of small
communities; Buena Vista, a grassroots organization of
"practitioners" from these communities; and the National
Alliance of Parishes, which comprises some 100 parishes
that are restructuring themselves into small communities.
Approximately 120 invited participants, including bishops, pastoral theologians, and representatives from as far
away as Hawaii, came together "to share their story of
living the Catholic life in Small Christian Community."[11]

Here is a sample of some of the most significant statements that were made at this consultation:

> We have convened at the invitation of the Notre Dame In-
> stitute for Pastoral and Social Ministry to share the story of
> our experience of living the Catholic life in small Christian
> communities.

It is our hope that some strategies could develop to encourage the building up of Catholic parish life in the United States and Canada.

We recognize our coming together at a momentous time in both the history of the world and the history of the Church.

We are in the time of a new Pentecost—a time of new beginnings. We need to be sensitive to the dynamic aspects of new life in its earliest stages.

To continue to promote what has emerged among us in these days we recommend the formation of a joint task force established by Buena Vista, the National Alliance of Parishes Restructuring into Communities, and the North American Forum for Small Christian Communities, to do the following: establish dialogue with the American bishops about the contribution of small Christian communities to parish life; pursue ways to continue the collaboration among these three groups and others who share this vision in a multicultural Church.

As this last recommendation is acted upon, an interface occurs between the aspirations of small communities and official statements from the Vatican. For example, on 30 January 1989, the Vatican released *The Apostolic Exhortation on the Mission of the Lay Faithful in the Church and in the World,* signed by Pope John Paul II, which implements the recommendations of the October 1987 world synod of the bishops on the laity. The *Exhortation* provides clear support for building ecclesial or small Christian communities throughout the Catholic world:

> So that all parishes . . . may be truly communities of Christians local ecclesial authorities ought to foster the . . . small basic or so-called "living" communities, where the faithful can communicate the Word of God and express it in service and love to one another. These communities are true

expressions of ecclesial communion and centers of evangelization, in communion with their pastors.

Concerning the formation of the lay faithful, encouragement is given: "Small Christian communities, where
present, can be a notable help in the formation of Christians, by providing a consciousness and an experience of
ecclesial communion and mission."

These sections are given further strength by their context within a discussion of an ecclesiology of communion.
The Vatican's Congregation for the Doctrine of the Faith
released in June 1992 a document that pays particular
attention to the interrelationship of Eucharist, community,
and the role of bishops in sustaining Church unity. This
document stresses the responsibility of Rome in contrast
to the contributions of regional Churches.

But one may ask, Is there a danger here that the Church
could be viewed too vertically with a heavy clericalism?
Another concern is that as laypersons assume greater responsibilities, the ordained may feel threatened, and tensions can easily develop; as the movement toward small
communities grows, some members of the clergy could
become apprehensive because laypersons would assume
roles of stronger leadership. Also, laypersons themselves,
in exploring new roles, can do so with some narrowness,
and a new type of elitism could emerge.

Will this participatory model lead eventually to official recognition that these communities are an essential
element of parish life? Are practice and theory coming
closer together? We do know that we live in a time of
new beginnings.

Rediscovering Community:
International Perspectives

Growing from this national gathering, an international
consultation took place at the University of Notre Dame

in December 1991 which manifested God's Spirit reaching out to and facilitating these communities throughout the world. Paulo Evaristo Cardinal Arns of Brazil said:

> The dynamism of participation and communion proposed by Puebla could be turned into a program not only for local Churches but for a project of evangelization of the whole of the Third World. There is a need for communion between the local Churches of the various regions of the world. The challenges of injustice and marginalization should bring these Churches to unite in charity among themselves.[12]

This communion among local Churches is reflected in what took place during the meeting. Christians from all walks of life—laity, religious, and clerics, women and men, married and single, Catholic and Protestant—from Bolivia, Brazil, Canada, Chile, England, France, Kenya, the Netherlands, Peru, Sierra Leone, Taiwan, Tanzania, and the United States entered into a vital community experience. They gathered to understand better each other's lived experience of small Christian communities, to appreciate mutuality and differences and to recommit their energies to the spread of the gospel. Each continental team shared stories of local communities and highlighted their achievements, struggles, and hopes. Communities acknowledged the experience of solidarity in faith and solidarity in human efforts to help bring about the reign of God in our world.

Like the first Pentecost described in Acts 2, each group from around the world heard others speak of the same "mighty acts of God" that enable all in this era of new Pentecost to recognize and respond to the signs of our times. In a world of dire poverty, ecological disaster, and escalating violence, these Christians realized anew the significance of "devoting themselves to the teaching of the apostles and to the communal life, to the breaking of the bread and to the prayers" (Acts 2:43). Strengthened in small communities in both First and Third World

Churches, they understand the cost of discipleship and have sometimes faced persecution and martyrdom in their efforts to share the "joys and hopes, the griefs and anxieties" of the modern world (*Gaudium et Spes,* 1). In a rediscovery of the social nature of Christian identity, they came to see that the Body of Christ is radically corporate, and that small Christian communities offer the world a way of recovering this realization.

Small Christian communities are a phenomenon in Christian Churches throughout the world. While Vatican II may not have foreseen a world-wide small community movement, the council and the movement are causally connected. Responsibility for proclaiming the Good News in the communities of Jesus Christ and to the world is a right and a duty rooted in baptism, and members of small Christian communities delight in the strong experience of truly being Church. In fact, in a number of countries, bishops' conferences have now made small Christian communities a top pastoral priority.

Community is the vocation of all Christians. In the opening Eucharist of the international consultation at Notre Dame, Bishop Christopher Mwoleka of Tanzania spoke of "a vocation to small Christian communities" in today's world and said that this is a vocation in which the laity are doing the leading. One of the characteristics of small Christian communities is that people take up leadership and ministry tasks according to their gifts, often with community discernment. Leadership functions from within the community and not from above it. Ministry and leadership are distributed throughout the Body of Christ. The small communities are a place where the roles of lay Christians are assuming new dimensions and definition. Because of the organic inherence of small Christian communities in the larger Church, this restructuring of roles calls for an assessment of many of the traditional roles played in leadership and in ministry.

Advances in biblical scholarship in the twentieth century have invited all Christian Churches to a repossession of their sacred texts. The Catholic retrieval of Scripture and the rapid evolution of a biblical spirituality are marks of the postconciliar Church. The living word of God is not just a text in Scripture. The text becomes the living word when it confronts contemporary human lives—individually and communally. Because God's word always addresses our lives today, social analysis facilitates our hearing of God's word. The word of God is in the world to help God's intentions to be realized in our historical circumstances. Just structures are to be celebrated, and unjust structures are to be transformed. Unjust structures cannot be changed by individuals but only by collective, connective presence and effort. (An African proverb tells us that enough spider webs woven together can stop a lion.) In all of the reports from small communities, a central place was given to the Bible: to study, to prayer, to discussion and interpretation, and to action in response to its word.

From this consultation several recommendations emerged, including that a network of ongoing communication and sharing of educational materials be set up; that the dialogue between grassroots leaders and clerical leaders be sustained and enlarged; that a more ecumenical climate be encouraged; that awareness of justice and peace issues be continuously facilitated; and that resource and training centers for leaders of small Christian communities be developed.

Following the consultation, participants traveled throughout the United States as guests of the Christian communities and at the invitation of some dioceses, where reports of their visits were recounted in diocesan papers. In November of 1992 a meeting was held at Notre Dame to explore ways to continue this networking. Then in August 1993 the three national organizations promoting Christian communities in the United States sponsored a national meeting in St. Paul, Minnesota, in order to encourage and develop further collaboration among themselves.

The 1993 joint convocation, which took place 5–8 August, had as its theme Creating Church for the Twenty-first Century." There were 425 participants, principally from the United States and Canada. The meeting was convened by the laity, and it was highly participatory. While the mood was hopeful, it was also realistic, with an awareness that difficult times are to be expected as the laity assumes greater responsibilities. Among the challenges are an increasing cultural diversity within the Church in the United States and the need for stronger collaboration from priests and bishops. All of the bishops of the United States were invited to the St. Paul meeting; only Archbishop John Roach, the local ordinary of Minneapolis–St. Paul was present at the opening ceremonies. On the other hand, more than thirty bishops committed themselves to take part in a workshop on small communities that was held just prior to the annual meeting of the U.S. bishops in November 1993.[13] This workshop fulfilled one of the goals of the 1990 National Consultation on Small Christian Communities, "thus establishing an avenue of dialogue among the laity, religious, and ordained about the small community experience as Church."[14]

All of this has led us in the United States to take seriously observations made by Robert Bellah on 18 January 1992:

Walter Brueggemann, one of our most interesting Old Testament scholars, has called the present situation in America an emergency. There are plenty of objective indicators that we are indeed in an emergency and the subjective perception of an emergency—a recent Gallup poll shows that over 70 percent of Americans think we have "gotten off the track"— is not to be taken lightly. . . . What is the nature of our emergency? Most obviously at the moment it is our economic situation, but it is clearly more pervasive, more systemic, than just economics. . . . We might be inclined to agree with former

President Vaclav Havel of Czechoslovakia when he said . . . : "The worst of it is that we live in a soiled moral environment. We have become morally ill because we are used to saying one thing and thinking another. We have learned not to believe in anything, not to care about each other, to worry only about ourselves. The concepts of love, friendship, mercy, humility or forgiveness have lost their depths and dimensions, and for many of us they represent only some sort of psychological curiosity or they appear as long-lost wanderers from faraway times, somewhat ludicrous in the era of computers and space ships." If we apply the concept of subsidiarity to the Church we can see it as calling for the animation of the whole body of Christ, right down to individual Christians, but including essentially the face-to-face groups that individuals always need to support them in performing activities vital to the life of the Church and to the witness of the Church in the world. Thus I think we can say that small Christian communities are not only legitimate as part of the life of the Church but essential to it.[15]

Thus we can say that whereas the small Christian communities are a worldwide phenomenon, the Church of the United States has been influenced especially by their origins and growth in Latin America. In the United States these groups are taking on their own form and identity. They have been strengthened by the communitarian sense of the Latin American Church.

Questions for Reflection

These questions were prepared by Michael and Barbara Howard, who live in Arvada, Colorado and have been members of a small Christian community for twenty-two years. They are cofounders of Buena Vista and were active participants in the National Consultation on Small Christian Communities (1990) and the International Consultation on Small Christian Communities (1991), both held at the University of Notre Dame. Barbara Howard has worked in two parishes that are developing small Christian communities, and she has served as national coordinator of Buena Vista.

1. The Latin American experience of small Christian communities indicates that individuals come to community out of a felt need. Generally speaking, the movement into small Christian communities in the United States is more prevalent among the middle class. What attraction does small Christian community hold for middle-class people?

2. Part of the "unfinished" agenda of the Second Vatican Council was its prescriptive definition of local Church as the diocese. What implication does that definition hold for the recognition of the small Christian community as a valid ecclesial expression? How can Scripture inform our ecclesial understanding of small Christian community?

3. Given that we are a nation of many cultures and diverse lifestyles, how can small Christian communities in the United States learn to be accepting and respectful of diverse cultural expressions? What can members of small communities learn from one another and from the larger world?

4. In understanding small Christian communities as a new Pentecost rather than a new Church program, what possible tensions arise in regard to ministry and leadership? Are the tensions real or perceived? Are there benefits from such tension?

5. What benefit would be achieved through a national or international network that could gather the "voice" of small Christian communities? How would that voice best be collected and to whom would it speak?

Notes

1. Christian Duquoc, *Liberation et progressime: Un dialogue théologique entre l'Amerique Latine et l'Europe* (Paris: Edition du Cerf, 1987).

2. Ibid.

3. Ibid.

4. Cf. Joseph Healey, M.M., "Today's New Way of Being Church," *International Papers in Pastoral Ministry,* University of Notre Dame, August 1990, vol. 1, no. 3; M. Azevedo, *Basic Ecclesial Communities,* (Washington, D.C.: Georgetown University Press, 1987).

5. This account about San Miguelito was provided through an interview with Professor Richard Westley of Loyola University in Chicago on 29 February 1992.

6. Richard Westley, *Good Things Happen: Experiencing "Community" in Small Groups* (Mystic, Conn.: 23rd, 1992), p. 138.

7. A complete report about this evangelization project can be obtained from Father Joseph F. Pawlicki, C.S.C., Nuestra Señora de Soledad Parish, 52–555 Oasis Palm Ave., Coachella, CA 92236.

8. "Evangelization," in the *Proceedings* of the second national meeting of dioscesan bishops (Washington, D.C.: United States Catholic Conference, Secretariat for Hispanic Affairs, 1977), n. 3, p. 68.

9. Nccb, *The Hispanic Presence: Challenge and Commitment* (Washington, D.C.: United States Catholic Conference, 1983).

10. "Evangelization," in *Proceedings,* p. 8.

11. "American Bishops Hear SCC Experiences," *Buena Vista Ink: The Newsletter of Buena Vista, Inc., a Network of People Devoted to the Formation and Support of Small Christian Communities,* January 1994, vol. 8, no. 1, p. 1.

12. Ligouri, Mo.: Ligouri Publications, 1980.

13. For further development of this joint convocation, see "Communities: New 'Way of Life,'" *National Catholic Reporter,* 27 August 1993; *International Papers in Pastoral Ministry,* University of Notre Dame, August–September 1993, vol. 4, no. 3.

14. "American Bishops Hear SSC Experiences," *Buena Vista Ink,* p. 1.

15. Robert N. Bellah, "Developing Small Christian Communities," remarks from Buena Vista Conference, Burlingame, Cal., 18 January 1992.

Suggested Reading

Aman, Kenneth, ed. *Border Regions of Faith, An Anthology of Religion and Social Change.* Maryknoll, N.Y.: Orbis, 1987.

Bellah, Robert N., et al. *The Good Society.* New York: Alfred A. Knopf, 1991.

Boff, Leonardo. *Ecclesiogenesis.* Maryknoll, N.Y.: Orbis, 1986.

Fitzpatrick, Joseph P. *One Church, Many Cultures: The Challenge of Diversity.* Kansas City, Mo.: Sheed and Ward, 1987.

Fraser, Ian. *Reinventing Theology as the People's Work.* Glasgow, Scotland: Wild Goose, 1988.

Jeffers, James S. *Conflict at Rome: Social Order and Hierarchy in Early Christianity.* Minneapolis: Fortress, 1991.

Lee, Bernard, and Michael Cowan. *Dangerous Memories.* Kansas City, Mo.: Sheed and Ward, 1986.

National Conference of Catholic Bishops. "Called and Gifted: Reflections on the American Bishops Commemorating the Fifteenth Anniversary of the Issuance of the Decree on the Apostolate of the Laity." *Origins* 10, 1980.

O'Halloran, James. *Signs of Hope: Developing Small Christian Communities.* Maryknoll, N.Y.: Orbis, 1991.

Rademacher, William J. *Lay Ministry: A Theological, Spiritual, and Pastoral Handbook.* New York: Crossroad, 1991.

5. SANTO DOMINGO

This dynamism of inculturation and evangelization
will be possible if we take seriously and translate into
all Church structures what the Santo Domingo document says about the laity as the first protagonists
in Gospel witness and preaching.
—*Paulo Evaristo Cardinal Arns*

Long before it began in October 1992, controversy surrounded the fourth general conference of Latin American
bishops in Santo Domingo, capital of the Dominican Republic. Would the bishops become embroiled in disputes
about the observance of the five-hundredth anniversary of
Columbus's arrival in the Americas? Would the pope find
himself used by Joaquin Balaguer when the president of
the Dominican Republic inaugurated his grandiose quin-
centennial lighthouse, a showpiece that projected a cross
miles into the skies?

Most importantly, would the bishops manage to own
their meeting and move forward with the vision of Medellín and Puebla? Those earlier conferences, held in 1968
and 1979, had laid the groundwork for applying the pastoral teachings of the Second Vatican Council to Latin
America and legitimized the pastoral option for the youth
and the poor of the hemisphere.

The roots of the 1992 conference go back to 1984,
when the council of Latin American bishops conceived
the idea of tying a conference to the anniversary of the
Columban voyages. A preliminary working document was

produced for critical reaction in 1990. Two revisions of that document yielded a version that many felt reflected the real concerns of the hemisphere's national Churches and pastoral groups. But the Vatican delayed its response until less than two months before the opening of the conference, thereby making it difficult for pastoral leaders to digest the response before the Santo Domingo sessions were upon them.

As the conference began, one could identify among the participants at least three different understandings of the teaching role of the Church: First, the "modern" mindset was accepting of the teachings of Vatican II but inclined to freeze these teachings in a historical moment; critics of this position felt it lacked an openness to developments since Vatican II had ended more than a quarter of a century ago. Second, the "centrist" group put emphasis on the directive role of the Vatican, and its members viewed the conference as a Roman meeting that happened to be taking place on Latin American soil. Third, the "liberating" wing tended to support such innovations as small Christian communities, liberation theology, and other popular Church movements in the region. While clearly acknowledging the role of central Church authority, this third group stressed the importance of listening to the grassroots; these participants viewed Santo Domingo primarily as a pastoral assembly of Latin American bishops.

The tension among these outlooks was obvious from the outset. Was the conference to be a type of synod, with its agenda and procedures determined by the Vatican's representatives? Or was it to be a gathering of Latin American bishops working in consultation with Vatican authorities? Before the meeting began, a manual had been prepared that called for a two-thirds vote on major decisions—a synodal approach. Then Rome named the Vatican secretary of state, Cardinal Angelo Sodana, as co-president of the meeting. In addition, the Vatican appointed as co-secretary general of the meeting Bishop Jorge Medina

Estevez of Chile, long a controversial figure among other key Chilean bishops. After consultation, the Vatican also named the chairs of the assembly's committees and appointed the facilitator for the gathering.

Despite everything, the conference turned out to be a genuine pastoral assembly of Latin American bishops. One of the key actors in that outcome was Archbishop Luciano Mendes de Almeida, S.J., president of the Brazilian conference of bishops and the chair of the conference's writing committee.

Shortly after the meeting opened, the basic working document was set aside and commissions went to work on four new drafts. The lengthy results of this process strayed a long way from the pastoral reality of Latin America. Dom Luciano then proposed that a new text—shorter and more concrete—be prepared by his writing committee. The proposal was accepted, chiefly out of respect for him.

Not even this committee's version was entirely satisfactory to the "liberating" group, but it was nonetheless accepted and approved, with the help of approximately five thousand amendments, as the assembly closed. Though a compromise, the statement was generally seen as providing a basis for moving the Church forward in Latin America.

One of the document's sources was the opening address of Pope John Paul II, in which he called for increased pastoral collaboration among the Americas, particularly in relation to justice and solidarity issues, and gave real encouragement to the development of such major conference themes as new evangelization, human promotion, and Christian culture. Another source was the working document of the conference, which clearly recognized the challenges facing the Church and made recommendations drawn from the social sciences together with theological reflection—in essence, representing the approach of liberation theology.

The list of official theologians did not include many well-known theologians. However, a number of these had contributed at various stages of the process. Some were elected representatives of their presbyterates. Others were given accreditation as religious journalists. A small and capable group took housing in Santo Domingo while they prayed and wrote drafts of interventions for interested bishops, working quietly and without seeking publicity. Some of them became "unofficial" theologians, and in this way assured their presence. They wrote articles on a daily basis for various newspapers throughout the world. They were not, however, used as fully as they could have been.

The official press conferences were held regularly at the Hotel Fiesta in Santo Domingo. Rapid and efficient communication was readily available to all who chose to use it. However, the tensions among the members of the conference were also evident in the press conferences. The press wanted clear information, which they did not feel was forthcoming. Some members of the press office were most helpful in making documentation available. The atmosphere improved significantly the day Paulo Evaristo Cardinal Arns of Brazil became an official panelist. Many trusted him to speak openly. At the end, journalists were invited to make a serious evaluation of the whole experience.

Parallel press conferences in another part of the city were sponsored by the Colectivo de Servicios Especiales de Comunicación (SEC). This service originates in Mexico City, and among its current representatives is José Alvarez Icaza who, along with his wife, was a lay auditor at the Second Vatican Council. SEC invited some "unofficial" theologians to serve as panelists. These theologians also prepared background papers for key issues of the conference. Experts in other fields, such as economics and the study of indigenous populations, were also represented. The SEC conferences had greater depth than the official ones, especially as they encouraged freer communication.

In his opening address, Pope John Paul II called for increased pastoral collaboration between the Americas, particularly as these related to justice and solidarity issues. In the final document, the participants—in the presence of representatives from the official United States and Canadian Catholic conferences—agreed to this proposal. At this moment the form it will take is not clear. For it to become a reality there will need to be in-depth pastoral research. The University of Notre Dame, through the agency of LANACC (Latin American/North American Church Concerns) of the Kellogg Institute, has volunteered to contribute to this effort along with other institutions of the Church. Areas for possible research would include the issue of the debt, the role of sects, ecological questions, and small Christian communities.

The conclusions of the conference put emphasis on a "new" way of evangelizing, not only within Latin America but also from that region out to other parts of the world. This approach reaffirms a preferential option for the poor and shows particular concern for indigenous peoples, Afroamericans, and youth.

The document adopted by the conference is a thing of lights and shadows. The lights include the fact that the assembly built on Medellín and Puebla, that it reaffirms a preferential option for the poor, that it contains a clear statement about women, and that it firmly supports small Christian communities. The shadows: Its treatment of sects and ecumenism is incomplete, it lacks a strong sense of the Church in the world, its Christology is abstract, and it shows real need for further research about economic issues.

In reflecting back upon the content and process of the Santo Domingo experience, one sees that the Latin American bishops stayed their course in spite of real challenges. The positive portions of the outcome may be partially due to luck, but in essence they are the result of perseverance and the workings of providence. The pastoral leaders of Latin America may now be in a position to move ahead with courage and creativity into the next century.

Questions for Reflection

1. The document of the conference at Santo Domingo is supportive of small Christian communities. Are these communities likely to experience even greater growth in years to come?

2. What new initiatives are necessary to strengthen ecumenism in the Americas?

3. "In the 1950s, a French Dominican, Father Perrin, wrote a famous book called *The Hour of the Laity*. In Latin America, that hour has come, has matured, and will produce fruits never dreamed of before" (Cardinal Arns). How may this influence the Churches of the Americas in the next century?

4. Do you think, along with Bishop Pedro Casaldáliga of Brazil, that we should shift our focus from a "new way of being Church" to a "new way of the Church being? What would each new path entail? Does one lead to the other?

Suggested Reading

For information concerning the documents and commentary on the Fourth General Conference of Latin American Bishops, see:

Hennelly, Alfred T., ed. *Santo Domingo and Beyond*. Maryknoll, N.Y.: Orbis, 1993.

AFTERWORD

The assembly of the Latin American bishops in Santo Domingo will come to be viewed as a real watershed in the life of the Churches in Latin America. This watershed originates in the opening discourse given by Pope John Paul II. He pointed to two perspectives that will incarnate the newness of evangelization in the coming years: First, evangelization has to give an answer to the worldwide crisis, a crisis never known before in history, a crisis that has to be answered in relation to the poor who have multiplied in the last decades and are being excluded from society. John Paul II states that today the poor are immersed in misery. Second, Pope John Paul II invites the Churches in the North and the South to unite, to face this crisis, and to offer alternatives for a new social order with new social models. For this reason, I repeat what I said after the assembly in Puebla: "The dynamism of participation and communion proposed by Puebla could be turned into a program not only for local Churches, but also for a project of evangelization for the whole of the Third World, and for the relationships between this and the Churches of the First World."

What can the Church in Latin America offer to her sister Churches in the North?

Liberation Theology

The Latin American Church can offer the union of efforts to solve the problem of poverty and misery on all levels of social life from the perspective of faith and *koinonia*. Liberation theology, from its origins, was based on a serious reading of biblical texts. It has been our experience in the United States, Canada, and Europe that this way of reflecting at the same time on God's word and on the suffering of the poor (who have increased dramatically in the First World also) seems to touch the mind and the hearts of all Christians more than abstract presentations on justice or social doctrine manage to do.

The Preferential Option for the Poor

A serious reading of the Bible leads us to see the identification that Yahweh (Amos 2:6–10; Jeremiah 22:16–17; Zephaniah 2:1–3) and Jesus (Matthew 11 and 25) make between a life of faith and the relation God's people have with their poor and oppressed. For us today this is a very complex problem. In the years since Medellín (1968) poverty has grown considerably in Latin America and in North America. Everyone is poorer than they were twenty-five years ago. Exactly at the moment that Latin America most needs help before hundreds of thousands die of malnutrition, North America is in worse of a condition than twenty-five years ago to be able to help.

John Paul II has called for a synod in which Churches of North and South can address the challenges of justice and solidarity. At this moment the Churches must work as equals.

Small Christian Communities

A new way of being Church. . . . We are challenged to present the newness of the gospel for our people today.

Twenty-five years ago the Church in Latin America tried to do this, uniting her people in small missionary communities that shared their faith, their daily lives, their sorrows, and the burden of a great social injustice. Through these decades the communities have grown, matured. Some have become installed as miniparishes and others have taken on the burden of participation in most of the popular movements that exist in Latin America.

Santo Domingo has offered them a new challenge. Inculturation is an appeal to the communities and to all the Church to make God's word constantly intelligible to all cultures, races, regions. Latin America (and North America) is rich in different cultures and races, different regional variations. We cannot speak to all women and men in the same words. Our new call to conversion is inculturation.

Lay Ministries

This dynamism of inculturation and evangelization will be possible if we take seriously and translate into all Church structures what the Santo Domingo document says about the laity as the first protagonists in gospel witness and preaching. Latin America made the happy experience of lay ministry on all levels. Women and men, young and old, rural and urban, have become the subjects of ministry. They preach, they preside at paraliturgies, they baptize, they witness weddings, they care pastorally for the ill and the dying, and for the spiritual well-being of the whole family in these difficult moments. They are ministers of the defense of human rights and of justice and peace. They work in ministries of alternative health care, housing, adult education, agrarian reform. Thousands of laypeople are studying in schools of faith for adults, in schools for ministry, and in undergraduate and graduate schools of theology. In the 1950s, a French Dominican, Father Perrin, wrote a famous book called *The Hour of the Laity*. In

Latin America, that hour has come, has matured, and will produce fruits never dreamed of before.

The Gift of Hope

The greatest gift that Christians can give each other is the gift of hope. Without it, love and faith are arid experiences. I honestly think, in these last decades as I have visited Canada, the United States, and Europe, that the gift Latin America has given to the North has been hope. We struggled to produce a theology that our people could relate to, we organized new ways of being the local Church (priorities, elected assemblies for decision making, integrated pastoral planning), we read the Scriptures starting from the lives of our people, we reorganized our seminaries in small houses of twelve students (as Jesus did with the disciples), women entered and illuminated every aspect of the life of the Church.

And we went to the North preaching the abundance of life we had found in our Churches. We touched your minds, your hearts, your very souls. You came South to work, to study, to research, to write books and articles about our experience, to do doctorates. You gave us of yourselves as we had done to you.

A new relationship has grown up. Thousands of Christians from North and South know each other as they never did before. They also love and respect each other. This had never happened before between continents. How many bishops are brothers to me! How many laypeople! From Penny Lernoux and Tom Fox whom I met as journalists, to my dear friends at the Catholic Worker House, to the universities that have received me as one of their own. When I celebrated twenty-five years as bishop I received letters of solidarity from such different people as Graham Greene and Ted Kennedy!

This hope that makes today and tomorrow beautiful is our gift to you and your gift to us.

We have your hope, you came to us and increased our hope.

PAULO EVARISTO CARDINAL ARNS
Archbishop of São Paulo, Brazil
27 March 1993

ABOUT THE AUTHOR

Robert S. Pelton, C.S.C., received both his licentiate and doctorate in theology from St. Thomas University, Rome. Presently Faculty Fellow at the Helen Kellogg Institute for International Studies at the University of Notre Dame, Pelton is also the editor of *International Papers in Pastoral Ministry* since 1991 and has published numerous articles focusing on the Catholic church and its future.

INDEX

Africa, 55
Ahuachapán, 41
Alinsky, Saul, 64
Allende, Salvador, 46
Alvarado, Pedro de, 38
Arns, Cardinal Paulo Evaristo, 2,
    71, 79, 85–89

Balaguer, President, 79
Battle, Helen, 9–17
Bellah, Robert, 374
"Border," ix
Bouvier, Virginia, 19–21
Brazil, 64
Brett, Edward, 21
Brueggemann, Walter, 74
Buena Vista, 68
Bush, President George, 42

Calero, Luis, 37, 61
Callahan, Judith, 9–17
"Call to Action," 26–27
CARA, 67
Carter, President Jimmy, 31
Casaroli, Agostino, 7, 9
Cátedra Nacional, 51, 52
CELAM IV, 4
Chile, 11, 14, 20, 46
Christian Men of San Miguelito,
    64
CICOP, 25

Cidai, 52
CLAR, 10, 13, 14
Communitarian, 18
Congregation of the Doctrine of
    the Faith, 70
Considine, John, 9
Cunningham, William, 9
Cushing, Cardinal, 64

de las Casas, Bartolomé, x
Del Valle, President, 30

Ecumenism, xiv, 30
Eldridge, Joseph, 20
El Salvador, 20, 28–29, 37f.;
    FMLN, 41–42; Peace Accords,
    33
Ellacuría, Ignacio, 49, 53
Elizondo, Virgilio, xv, 5
Encomienda, 39

Fox, Tom, 88
Friedman, Richelle, 22

Galvez, Luis, 9
Gaudium et spes, 72
Gleason, Theresa, 9–16
Gomez, Bishop, xv
Grande, Rutilio, 47
Greene, Graham, 88
Greisgraber, Jo Marie, 20

Guatemala, 40

Havel, Vaclav, 75
Hehir Bryan, 26
Hennelly, Alfred T., 84
Hickey, Cardinal, 28
Higgins, George, 26
*Hispanic Presence: Challenge and
    Commitment,* 67
Hispanics in U.S., xiii, 18, 66ff.
Hoban, Anne, 9–11, 13–18
Houlihan, Margaret, 9–17
Howard, Michael and Barbara,
    75
Hoye, Monsignor Daniel, 28

Icaza, José Alvarez, 82
Idhuca, 52
Institute for Pastoral and Social
    Ministry, 68
International Consultation, 70ff.
International Papers, 21
Irarrazaval, Diego, 2
Iudop, 52

Jesuits, xv, 28, 37, 47
John Paul II, Pope, 69, 81–85
Joint Convocation, 73ff.

Kellogg Institute, 83
Krol, Archbishop John, 26

Laboa, Bishop José, 32–33
LANACC, 83
Latin American Bishops, xv, 4,
    25, 38, 79, 85
LaVoy, Diane, 20
Law, Cardinal Bernard, 28
Lernoux, Penny, 88
Lewers, William, 66
Liberation Theology, 63, 86

Maher, Bishop Leo, 66
Mahon, Leo, 64

Mahony, Cardinal Roger, 33
Malone, Bishop James, 28
Martyred women, xv, 21, 49
McCarthy, Jo Ellen, 9–17
McGovern, Eileen, 9–16
McGovern, James, 6, 22
McGrath, Archbishop Marcos,
    29–31
Medellín, xv, 4, 8, 18, 25, 27,
    43ff., 83
Medina, Bishop Jorge, 80
Mendes de Almeida, Archbishop
    Luciano, 81
Mexico, ix, 9
Moakley, Joseph, 22
Mwoleka, Bishop, 62, 72

NACPR, 68
NAFTA, xi
Nangle, Joseph, 9–18
National Consultation, 68, 74
NCCB, 67
Nicaragua, 12, 20, 28, 46
North American Forum, 68
Noriega, 29, 30, 33

OAS, 9, 32
Option for the poor, 44, 49, 86

Panama Bishops Conference
    (CEP), 29ff.
Pawlicki, Joseph, 66
Pelton, Robert, 9–17
Pfeifer, Bishop Michael, 9–16
Pilarczyk, Archbishop Daniel, 29,
    33
Pinochet, Augusto, 46
Poverty, 55
Priests of Holy Cross, 66
Puebla, xv, 27, 44ff., 83

Quigley, Thomas, 19
Quinn, Archbishop, 27

Ramírez, Bishop Ricardo, ix–xvi, 27
Rausch, Bishop James, 26
Reagan, President Ronald, 20
Realidad nacional, 38, 50
Religious-based grassroots communities, 21–22
Religious communities of U.S., 3
Renewing the Earth, xii
Repartimiento, 39
Rivera y Damas, Archbishop Arturo, 28
Roach, Archbishop, 74
Romero, Archbishop Oscar, xv, 21, 31, 46ff., 52

Salmon, Sheila, 9–17
Santa Ana, 41
Santa Clara U., 58–60
Santo Domingo, xv, 79, 83–87
Scowcroft, Brent, 28
Second Religious Congress of the U.S., 7
SEC, 82
Society of St. James, 64

Sodano, Cardinal, 80
Sununu, John, 28

Universidad Centro-Americana (UCA), 4, 37ff.
University of Notre Dame, 7, 9, 21, 68, 70, 83
Uruguay, 20
U.S. Bishops, 25, 27, 28, 33, 67, 74
USCC, 26, 27

Valley Missionary Program, 66
Van Kleef, Nicholas, 31
Vatican II, 2, 25
Vatican Documents: *Letter to Bishops*, 1; *Apostolic Exhortation*, 69
Waldron, Edward, 32
Westley, Richard and Ethel, 4, 5, 65
White, Robert, 22
Wipfler, William, 19
WOLA, 19–21